PERFORMANCE EVALUATION OF UNIVERSITY LIBRARIES

PERFORMANCE EVALUATION OF UNIVERSITY LIBRARIES

An Application of Cost-Effectiveness Analysis

M. Surya and S. Balakrishnan

KALPAZ

Performance Evaluation of University Libraries : An Application of Cost-effectiveness Analysis

ISBN: 978-81-7835-906-9

Published in 2012 in India by
Kalpaz Publications
C-30, Satyawati Nagar,
Delhi-110052
E-mail: kalpaz@hotmail.com
Phone : 9212729499

Lasser Type Setting by: Rudra Computer Graphics, Delhi
Printed at : Chawla Offset Press, Delhi

Contents

List of Tables

Chaper 9

Chapter 9

1

Introduction

India of unique characteristics of having the third largest system of higher education (next to the USA and USSR) in the world. There are 130 Universities, 16 deemed Universities, 5482 colleges and 11 institutions of national importance in the country. These institutions enrol 3.5 million students for graduate, postgraduate and research degrees and diplomas and employ 228 thousand teachers for teaching and research. With the spread of higher education in India through the planning era, the libraries have been looked upon as an important adjunct to education.

The University Grants Commission has opined that the library is the core of an University. As a resource, it occupies the central and primary place because it serves all the functions of a University-teaching and research, the creation of new knowledge and the transmission posterity of the learning and culture of the presentand the past.

(A) Aims and Objectives of University Education

The system of University Education in India has undergone different stages of development from mere workshops for the "production" of subordinate staff to centres of advanced learning and research. The objectives of an Indian University during the pre-independence period had been to strive to achieve the goals that were set by foreigners to promote their own interests.

The earliest Universities of modern India, i.e., Calcutta, Madras and Bombay, all founded in 1857, were established not for the advancement of learning and research but to conduct examinations and award degrees as a hallmark of fitness for recruitment to the civil service of the country. However in 1950s, it was felt that the purpose of education is not indoctrination but the development of the power to form sound judgments. Pandit Jawaharlal Nehru, late Prime Minister of India, in his convocation address at the University of Allahabad in December 1947, summed up the basic objectives of the University and its role in national life as: "A University stands for humanism, for tolerance, for reason, for the adventure of ideas and for the search of truth. It stands for the onward march of the human race towards even higher objectives." The University Education Commission which was formed under the Chairmanship of Dr. S. Radhakrishnan (1948-49) elucidates the aims of University education in the post-independent India as: "The education system must find its guiding principle in the aims of a social order for which it prepares, and in the nature of the civilisation it hopes to build. Democracy depends for its very life on a high standard of general, vocational and professional education. Dissemination of learning, incessant search for new knowledge, unceasing effort to plumb the meaning of life, provision for professional education to satisfy the occupational needs of our society are the vital tasks of higher education." With the rapid changes in the socio-economic structure of the country, the Universities are also undergoing profound changes in their scope, functions and organisation. They are in a process of evolution. Their tasks are no longer confined to the two traditional functions of teaching and advancement of knowledge.

They are assuming new functions and the older ones are increasing in range, depth and complexity. In broad terms, the functions of the Universities in the modern world may be said to be the following:

(i) To seek and cultivate new knowledge, to encourage vigorously and fearlessly in the pursuit of truth, and to interpret old knowledge and beliefs in the light of new needs and discoveries,

(ii) To provide the right kind of leadership in all walks of life, to identify gifted youth and help them develop their potential to the full by cultivating physical fitness, developing the powers of the mind and cultivating right interests, attitudes and moral and intellectual values,

(iii) To provide society with competent men and women trained in agriculture, arts, medicine, science and technology and various other professions, who will also be cultivated individuals, imbibed with a sense of social purpose,

(iv) To strive to promote equality and social justice and to reduce social and cultural differences through diffusion of education and

(v) To foster in the teachers and students and, through them, in society generally, the attitudes and values needed for developing the good life in individuals and society.

The National Education Conference held at *Sevagram* on 15th October 1972 has reset the goals of education, viz., (i) self-reliance, self-confidence and dignity of labour through the use of work as an integral part of educational programme; (ii) a spirit of nationalism and social-responsibility through involvement of students, and teachers in a meaningful programme of community service; and (iii) inculcation of ethical and moral values and proper understanding of the essential unity of all religions.

Universities have assumed a significant role in research and development in recent times. They become the training ground for the development of human resources and pivotal in the production of sophisticated manpower in adequate numbers to deal creatively with new technologies.

(b) Role of University Libraries

Keeping in view these objectives, the University library system has to undertake many responsibilities and perform varied functions. The prime necessity for University is a well established library with a balanced and adequate collection, which can satisfy the needs of the University faculties and support the instructional and research programmes. A University is rated largely by its library. No University can develop and implement the academic activities successfully without a strong library at its centre. The Radhakrishnan Commission observed that the library is the heart of all the University work". It is from this that the entire teaching and research activities should radiate. In the words of S.R. Dongerkery, "A well-stocked and up-to-date library is a sine qua non for every modern University[11]. It is the central workshop of the University which provides the student, the teacher, and the research worker with the tools required for the advancement of knowledge. It is obvious that the library exists with a view to and for the sake of the University; it is an instrument which helps to realise the academic objectives according to the standards of the general policy and functions of the University body itself.

The Kothari Commission on Education (1964-66) insists that the University Library should,

(i) provide resources necessary for research in fields of special interest to the University;

(ii) aid the University teacher in keeping abreast of development in his field;

(iii) providelibrary facilities and services necessary forthe success of all formal programmes of instruction;

(iv) open the doors to thewide world of books that lie beyond the borders of one's own field of specialization, and

(v) to bring books, students, and scholars together under coordination which encourage reading for pleasure, self-discovery, personal growth, and the sharping of intellectual curiosity.

The Association of Indian Universities has enumerated the objectives of University Libraries as below:

(i) To support the teaching and research programmes of the University;

(ii) To develop its collection by acquiring necessary reading materials to meet the present and future needs of its users for whom it is meant;

(iii) To organise its collection, operations and services so as to provide for the reading materials and information needs of its users in anticipation and on demand. Net working and resource sharing among University Libraries should be practised by each institution towards utilisation of all resources;

(iv) To introduce, if necessary, technological innovations like computer/word processors etc. to facilitate users getting prompt service;

(v) To provide facilities like reprography, inter library loans and translation and documentation to assist the users;

(vi) To promote library user education and relate to technological innovations so that the academic librarian will no longer remain a craft man but serving educationalist through technological means;

(vii) Towards achieving the above goals, to get adequate finances staff, storage and other facilities;

(viii) Maximise efficiency of services with reference to inputs/ expenditure so as to make library services cost-effective.

The factors essential for the successful operation of the library may be grouped under:

(i) resources for instruction, research and extension,
(ii) a team of competent library staff,
(iii) organisation of materials for use,
(iv) adequate space and equipment,
(v) integration of the library with administrative and educational policies,
(vi) integration of the library with the community, state, regional, national and international library resources,
(vii) adequate financial support, and
(viii) a workable policy of library government.

Thus, it is realised that the Library is an integral part of an institution of higher learning and it plays a significant role in the academic life of the University. It is considered not only as the nerve centre of the educational institution but also the heart which circulates the thought-energy to the workers in the fields of humanities, social sciences, Engineering & Technology. Any University with an outstanding library can have an extremely valuable advantage over other institutions in holding the best scholars and teachers within its folds. It is also realised that only through the efficient functioning of the library, the academic programmes of the University can be implemented successfully. This, in turn, depends upon, (i) the availability of relevant collection, (ii) adequate number of efficient staff members and (iii) other infrastructural facilities.

For this purpose, provision of adequate funds is of central importance to the Library. Besides, the funds alloted to the library is to be distributed/allocated in such a way as to maximise the effectiveness of the library performance. This requires periodical evaluation of the effective allocation, efficiency of operation and improvements in performance.

(c) Problems Faced by the University Libraries

In recent years, the problems faced by the University Libraries have become complex and varied. Particularly, they have been very much pressurised by both the internal and external factors. 'The internal factors imply the demand aspect. For instance, the demands made on the libraries have been increasing rapidly in the past two decades, consequent on the introduction of new research programmes, socially relevant projects, job-oriented courses and the expansion of Research and Development in almost all subject fields. The external factors indicate the economic and financial aspect. Especially, the academic libraries are experiencing severe financial problems which may be ascribed to the extraordinary increase in :

(i) the cost of library materials; (ii) wages and salaries of the staff* and (iii) building, furniture and equipment cost.

The financial problems of the libraries are made still more severe due to the (i) increasing volumes of publications, (ii) development of new library services, (iii) expansion of existing

* Libraries as all other institutions and organizations in the public and private sectors, are faced with the economic problem of allocating their limited resources in such a manner as to generate in maximum benefits. In this context, they are under increasing pressure not only to specify their needs or required 'inputs', but to indicate in some meaningful and measurable way, what their 'outputs' are.
Both the impact of inflation and the declining money valuc have contributed to the escalating material cost. *Over* the last five years, the annual increase in monographs has been 10 percent and periodicals 11 percent.

library services, (iv) phenomenal increase of user population, (v) extension of instructional programmes and (vi) introduction of new programmes. These factors have contributed to the magnitude of financial crisis faced by the University Libraries. As a result, the cost of library expenditure have soared up rapidly.*

While the demand for library funds has been growing alarmingly, the budgetary provisions made for the University Libraries are stagnant and the sources of finance are too limited.** This conflicting tendencies have to be resolved properly, otherwise it will affect the basic survival of the libraries as essential parts of the University education system besides eroding the viability of the library services.

This has posed an inevitable challenge to the University Libraries in striking out a balance between these two pressures, viz., (i) the ever growing demands on the oneside and (ii) the financial stringency and the persistent escalation of library cost on the other. The existing situation has forced the University Librarians to evaluate the performance of the various units of the library*** so as to identify (i) the internal operational efficiency and (ii) the effectiveness of the overall performance.

(d) Setting

The basic problems faced by the University library are (i) obtaining adequate allotment of funds from the University

---

* Baumol and Marcus (1973) have identified the annual growth rate of salaries and wages as 9.7 percent.

** Most of the University Libraries have failed to meet the expectations of the readers and they have to put up with a lot of imperfections from practically ail quarters and as such are not effective as one would wish. This is due to the lack of funds and the improper utilisation of the given grants.

*** Since the early 1970's Libraries have been experiencing a sub-stantial loss of their standard of living as a result of stringent budget and double-digit inflation.

Budget, University Grants Commission and other sources, and (ii) harmonising the funds among library materials, personnel and physical facilities so as to balance the resources and requirements.

Thus, there are two aspects of the problem of library performance, viz., (i) problems associated with the allotment of funds and (ii) problems related to the allocation of funds among the various input items.* The first problem involves analysis of the allotment of funds on sound criteria and its adequacy in tune with requirements i.e., rising cost and growing demands. The second problem entails evaluation of the effect of allocation of funds among the various input items in terms of operational efficiency and effective performance.

Any study of performance has, therefore, to probe into the following factors:

(1) Whether the library fund is dequate to support the growing academic programmes of the University.

(2) How well the funds are allocated to meet the requirements of the users.

(3) Is the operational efficiency of the Acquisition, Technical and Service Units Optimal.

---

* Libraries, rather late in the day, are coming round to measuring their level of performance rather than just the *level* of their inputs in order to (i) assess the extent to which the library resources and services are meeting the demands of the clientele and to (ii) demonstrate to top management that the resources are being used effectively.

** Nearly three-fourths of the University Libraries in India have faced the problem of 'non-correspondence' between the resources and requirements. This imbalance could, therefore, be solved by efficient allocation of resources among the input items in the order of their contribution to the performance.

(4) How well the library resources (materials) and Services are utilised in terms of cost-effectiveness of performance.

(5) To make a comparative study ofthe cost-effectiveness of the performance of the University Libraries in Tamil Nadu.

(e) Statement of the Problem

The present study, therefore, aims at analysing the performance of two University Libraries in Tamil Nadu viz: Annamalai University Library and Madurai Kamaraj University Library. Among the existing ten University Libraries in the State, only these two libraries have been functioning for a period of more than twenty years and hence they have been selected for the purpose of analysis.* The study attempts to evaluate the performance of the library services in terms of cost effectiveness analysis. The three essential units of the library viz: (i) Acquisition Unit, (ii) Processing Unit and (iii) Service Unit are taken up for analysis.

(f) Concepts Performance Measure

PM refers to the contribution made by the various sections of the library in the form of tangible or intangible outputs to its patron or parent organisation. PM helps to identify (i) what is being accomplished in each unit, (ii) what is their level of performance in terms of standards or norms, (iii) which of the activities/operations fail to contribute to the attainment of goals, (iv) what are the factors affecting the performance and (v) how to take corrective or remedial action.**

Cost-Effectiveness Analysis: The various techniques adopted to measure the library performance include: (i) Library

---

* Out of the remaining 8 University libraries except Madras University Library, others are of very recent origin and they have yet to take off their ground.

** PM helps to find the strength and limitation of each unit of the library and thereby assists in decision-making and future planning.

Effectiveness analysis, (ii) Cost Benefit analysis, (iii) Cost-Efficiency analysis and (iv) Cost-Effectiveness analysis. Among these techniques, "Library Effectiveness" focusses on the extent to which library.' outputs meet the requirements of its user community. In otherwords, it explains the contributions of the library to its clientele or to the parent institution. This method takes into account mostly the returns/outputs and ignores the input aspect/cost aspect.*

On the contrary, the "cost-benefit" evaluation implies the measurement of the returns in terms of cash. But most of the outputs of the libraries cannot be measured in monetary terms. Hence, it is not applicable to the present study.

The other method is "cost-efficiency". It refers to the maximisation of the effectiveness of spending, regardless of the effectiveness in terms of stated objectives or performance criteria. Cost-efficient spending implies the elimination of wasteful operations to achieve a given level of output at minimum cost. It does not necessarily maximize the performance.

In view of the above, the most scientific method is cost-effectiveness analysis. It deals with the relationship between the cost incurred on the different Units of the library and the level of performance derived from them. This method is used to examine the library system with a view to improve their cost-effectiveness, either by achieving the same objective at a lower cost or by more fully achieving the objectives for the same cost. The cost-effective library is seen as the desirable condition, providing the highest level of performance, consistent the given level of expenditure and resource consumption.

---

* Until we have measures of both costs and effectiveness, it is obvious that we cannot manage a library system in a way that will minimise costs and maximise effectiveness.

CEA provides the Librarians a diagnostic procedure just like other forms of diagnosis. It is intended to lead to therapeutic action leading to significant improvement in the performance of the system.

Notes

1. Association of Indian Universities. *Universities Handbook* (1985-86): Diamond Jubilee Edition, New Delhi: Association of Indian Universities, 1985. p. 2.

2. University Grants Commission (1968-69). *Report*. pp. 1-2.

   In: C.G. Viswanathan. *University Libraries of India: Principles and Policy.* New Delhi: C.G. Viswanathan, 1972. pp. 5-6.

3. University Grants Commission, "Capital provision for University Libraries: Report of a working party" London: HMSO, 1976. In: Norman Higham *The Library in the University.* London: Andre Deutsch, 1980. p. 11.

4. S.R. Ranganathan. "University Libraries Then and Now" *Library Herald,* 6:1963. p. 62.

5. Zakir Hussain. Convocation address at University of Utkal, Cuttack, December 6, 1959.

6. Report of the Education Commission, 1964-66: *Education and National Development*, p. 274.

---

* Cost-effectiveness - Maximize output at a given level of cost (output-oriented) (not necessarily the least-cost solution). Cost-efficiency - Minimize cost at a given level of output (input-oriented) (not necessarily the most effective solution in terms of goals or performance)
Cost-efficiency does not necessarily relate to the maximum level of performance desired. However, cost-effectiveness is usually consistent with a high level of cost-efficiency.

7. India, University Education Commission (1948-49) (Chairman: S. Radhakrishnan).'Report.2v' Delhi: Manager of Publications, GOI, 1949. pp. 35-67.

8. India, Education Commission (1964-66) (Chairman: D.S. Kothari). Educational planning and the National policy. Delhi: NCERT,1971.

9. *Hindustan Times,* 17.7.72.

10. India, Ministry of Education. *Challenge of Education: a policy perspective.* August 1985, p. 80.

11. India, University Education Commission. (1948-49) op.cit., p. 110.

12. S. R. Dongerkery."Libraries in University Education". In: N. N. Gidwani (Ed.) *Comparative Librarianship.* Delhi: Vikas, 1973. p. 15.

13. HJ. De Vleeschauwer. "University Library: Its Nature and Functions". *Mousion,* Vol. 59; 1963. p. 35.

14. India, Education Commission (1964-66). op.cit., p. 521.16.

15. Association of Indian Universities. "National policy on University Libraries", *Report.* New Delhi: AIU, 1985.

16. Louis Round Wilson and Maurice F. Tauber. *The University Library,* 2nd ed., New York: Columbia Press, 1956. p. 15.

17. Rosemary Ruhig Dumont and Paul F. Dumont, "Measuring Library Effectiveness: A Review and an Assessment", *Advances in Librarianship,* 9, New York: Academic Press, 1979.

18. Frederick C. Lynden."Library Materials Budgeting in the Private University Library: Austerity and Action". *Advances in Librarianship,* 10, New York: Academic Press, 1980. p. 96.

19. Hugh F. Ciine, *Building Library collections.* Toronto: D. C. Health and Company, 1981. p. 72.

20. Thomas 3. Waldhartand Thomas P. Marcum. "Productivity Measurement in Libraries". *Advances in Librarianship,* 6, New York: Academic Press, 1976. p. 54.

21. Stephen A. Roberts. Cost management for library and information services. London: Butterworths, 1985. p. 6.

22. S.N. Srivastava and S.C. Verma. *University Libraries in India.* New Delhi: Sterling Publishers, 1980. pp. 12-13.

23. Richard De Gennaro. "Austerity, technology and resource sharing: research libraries face the future". *Library Journal,* 100, 1975. pp. 917-923.

24. Ross Shimmon (Ed.) *A Reader in Library Management*, London: Clive Bingley, 1976. pp. 162-165.

25. S.N. Srivastava and S.C. Verma. op.cit., p. 13.

26. Edward Evans, Harold Borko and Patricia Ferguson."Review of Criteria used to measure library effectiveness". In: Ross Shimmon *(Ed.) A Reader in Library Management.* London: Clive Bingiey, 1976. p. 164.

27. John Martyn and F. Wilfred Lancaster. *Investigative Methods in Library and Information Science: an introduction.* Virginia: Information Resources Press, 1981. p. 183.

2

Review of Literature

Measuring the performance of the academic libraries is of recent origin. This has been warranted by the (i) soaring of the library expenditure due to the increasing (a) cost of library materials, (b) personnel and (c) physical facilities and (ii) heavy increase in (a) user population, (b) number of academic and research programmes and (c) publication. The rise in prices on the one side and demand for more materials on the other have affected the continued viability of the library services. This has necessitated effective allocation of funds among the input items so as to derive better services within the available infrastructure.

(a) General Performance Measures

A plethora of studies have been attempted on the issue of evaluating the library performance in terms of (a) allocation efficiency and (b) operational effectiveness. Among the existing studies to assess the allocation efficiency of the library, some have suggested standards such as (i) per capita library expenditure, (ii) book stock per user population, (iii) lower cost per item held, (iv) circulation per capita, (v) cost per loan transaction etc. Regarding operational effectiveness criterion such as (i) cost, (ii) Accessibility, (iii) user satisfaction, (iv) response time, (v) cost/benefit ratio and (vi) use, etc. have been suggested for evaluation.

Based on these approaches, the studies could be broadly under three distinct measures such as (i) allocative efficiency, (ii) availability and (iii) utility. Among these three approaches, the 'allocative efficiency[1], refers to the achievement of maximum out put at a given level of cost. This approach has been advocated by Lancaster, Knightly and Duchesne. According to Lancaster and Climension a retrieval system is to be evaluated strictly in terms of user satisfaction. That is, the operating efficiency is to be evaluated from the point of view of satisfying user requirements and efficiency. Such evaluation however, involves a determination of whether or not the cost of operating libraries are justified by the benefits derived from it.

The authors have taken into consideration such variables as, coverage, usability, recall, precision, response time and user effort for evaluating the efficiency of the total library systems. The basic steps involved in the cost-effectiveness analysis of the libraries include (i) identifying the objectives of the library, (ii) designing the alternative methods of meeting these objectives, (iii) determination of the costs of these various alternatives, (iv) establishing one or more models that relate the costs of each alternative to an assessment of the extent to which each could assist in obtaining these objectives and (v) establishing a criteria for ranking the alternatives in the order of desirability and choosing the most promising.

The authors have also suggested methods to improve the effectiveness of the library performance. They include (i) maintaining the present performance level while reducing the costs operating the system and (ii) holding operating cost constant while raising the average performance level.

The evaluation of library performance has been concerned with the major issues such as (i) effort evaluation focussing on (ii) process evaluation focussing on the appropriateness efficiency of activities and programmes, (iii) effectiveness on the extent to which outputs accomplish organizational objectives and (iv) impact evaluation focussing on the extent to which accomplished objectives actually meet the needs of the parent organization. The model suggested by Knightly[2] also includes user's opinion, expert's opinion, formulas, standards, comparison to other organization quantifiable operations, outputs and costs.

Duchesne[3] has delineated a budgetary model taking into consideration the direct and indirect cost involved inthe various library programmes such as acquisition, cataloguing, circulation, reprography, reference and administration. Against these input factors should be presented the output units such as number orders, number of titles catalogued, number of volumes loaned, number of pages photocopied, number of readers and number of employees. From the unit cost calculated, the future costs and operations has to be decided.

"Availability approach" indicates the evaluation of the performance of the library in terms of (a) financial provision and (b) collection development. This parameter has been suggested by Revill[4], CLIM[5], Sewell[6] and Hannubuss[7].

Measures of 'availability' are advocated as performance academic libraries by Revill[4]. The variables used to calculate the probability of availability include the number of terms (a) acquired, (b) processed, (c) circulated and (d) the number success served. Questionaire method is used to test the library's success and failure providing the wanted items. This study helps to discover the reasons why books are not always readily available. The results can be used in book fund allocation, selection of stock and improving library operations.

The Centre for Library and Information Management has adopted 'availability technique' to find out the incidence of 'system failure' and 'reader failure.[4] It is used to identify the genuine absence the book from the shelf and the reader's in aptitude at finding the book.

The availability of (i) book stock per head of population, (ii) annual addition to stock, (iii) per capita library expenditure, (iv) proportion of qualified staff and (v) provision of space have been suggested by Sewell to assess the library performance.

Hannubuss has suggested that availability, utilisation, adequacy and unit cost may be taken as parameters to test the performance of the library.

The "utility approach" indicates that the library resources and services must be easily accessible to the reader, so that they can be put to maximum use. This approach has been recommended by Hamburg[5], Ladendorf, Zweizig, Rzasa and Baker, Pings and Dumont et. al.

Hamburg[6] has recommended 'utilization[7] as a measure library performance, which reflects the capability of the library to the User's requirements, and it is based on document or usage of library materials. The methods used by et. al. to evaluate the document exposure include (i) exposure and its (ii) item use days. The first method is to count each circulation, each direct in-library use, each inter-library loan, indirect exposure as one unit of exposure. The second method entails counting "item use-days". This measure differs from the counting of exposures because a long circulation involving exposure during x different days is counted as x items use-days rather than as exposure. The second method has the advantage of using a common unit of measurement across exposure types.

The overall performance is evaluated by matching with the exposures occurring in any period of time, the costs of facilities, equipment, resources, staff and other services necessary to produce are exposure. The criteria suggested for evaluation is exposure hours per dollar.

The average rate of document usage per fixed time has[8] recommended by Ladendorf[9] as a device for measuring the effectiveness of library operations. The variables that influence this measure are the cost of operation and the usage rate itself, as well as the total managerial structure of the library.

The approaches to the measurement of library use enumerated by Zweizig[10] include (i) measuring use, (ii) measuring users and (iii) measuring uses. To measure the use of the system the factors such as (a) number of books circulated, (b) number of inter-library loan requests filled, and (c) the number of reference questions answered have been taken into consideration. The variables such as (a) the frequency of attendance at the library, (b) percentage of population served, (c) number of registered borrowers and (d) the persons actually borrowing materials have been taken into account to measure the proportion of users and non-users of a library. To measure the library uses, the user satisfaction or the extent of utilisation of the library is taken into consideration.

Thus, measurement of use provides information on the quantity of activity or the output of the library operations. The measurement of users reveals the nature of the clientele. The measurement of uses exhibits the functional contribution of the library in terms of impact.

---

* Library effectiveness may also be evaluated by its usage. Here, Murphy has adopted survey method to measure the amount of utility. The variables suggested by him include (i) the comfort and attractiveness of the surroundings and the quality of the study atmosphere; (ii) the physical access to library collection; (iii) the helpfulness, efficiency and friendliness of the reference and cirçulation staff; (iv) the availability of other services; (v) the adequacy of the resources; (vi) the reasons for using the library and (vii) the frequency of use. A five point scale has been used to analyse the responses.

Source: (Mercy Murphy, "Measuring Library effectiveness". *Special Libraries*, Jan. 1979; pp. 18-25.

Another measure to evaluate the impact of library programmes on the users has been suggested by Rzasa[11] and Baker. The criteria established for the primary measures are (i) the number of material items utilised, (ii) the number of actual users, (iii) the number of information items sought, (iv) the number of satisfactory information items received and (v) the area of study space utilized. The total population served is used as a basis for the primary measures, other words, changes in the user population served should be taken into account.

The criteria established for the secondary measures are (i) the number of actual users from a given sub-population and (ii) the return rate of these users. The sub-population which the library served is used as a basis for the secondary measures.

The Institute for the Advancement of Medical Communication[12] has developed methods for testing the ability of an academic library to provide specific services. These include the ability to deliver books and journals, to supply answer of simple fact, and to deliver documents through inter-library lending.

The criteria for measuring library effectiveness that has been suggested by Dumont[13] and et.al., includes such factors as (i) goal achievement as measured by contributions to its patrons, (ii) the optimization of performance, (iii) the degree of user satisfaction, (iv) the use of human resources and (v) the ability to serve the users.

(b) Evaluation of the Performance of the Acquisition Unit

The main target of the Acquisition Unit is to develop a judicious collection of library materials keeping in view of the

---

* As the library collections form the base of the entire library activity, this section should take more care to develop a (i) comprehensive, (ii) balanced, (iii) adequate and (iv) efficient collection which will satisfy the recreational informational, educational and research needs of the undergraduates, graduates, researchers, staff members and administrators of the University.

diversified information requirements of the students, researchers and staff members.* The allocation of funds to this unit must based on both the internal and external factors.** The performance : must be assessed in terms of (i) Adequacy of allotment and (ii) Effectiveness of collection.

(i) Adequacy of Allotment

A review of the existing studies bring to light : that the adequacy of the book-budget alloted have to be judged by taking into account such factors as (i) user's strength, (ii) instructional and research programmes introduced, (iii) requirements, of the individual departments, (iv) cost of publications, (v) size % of the existing collection and (vi) utilisation of the collection.

Here, Burton[1] has suggested (i) weighted users, (ii) mono and serials needed per weighted user, (iii) average cost 'monograph and serials, (iv) volumes to be bound and (v) average cost per volume to be bound as the basis for the projection of book fund requirements in academic and research libraries.

Drake[2] has recommended usage-based allocation methods for universities that is based on the number and diversity of instructional and research programmes. He has emphasised the factors that are to be taken into consideration viz., (i) the size of the library budgt relative to the university total budget, (ii) diversity instructional programme and (iii) the philosophy of the university management.

Weiwood[3] has suggested such variables as enrollment, circulation and courses offered for allocating book-budget. According to him, priority has to be assigned to the Departments where these variables are found in large number.

** The internal factors include the (i) growing student population, introduction of new instructional and research programmes and (ii) the expansion of research etc. The external factors include the (i) literature explosion and (ii) the rising cost of publication etc.

The factors that are to be given weight in allocating book-fund for each subject are detailed by Lewis[4]. They are (i) under graduate credit-person hours, (ii) number of undergraduate majors, (iii) graduate credit-person hours, (iv) number of graduate majors, (v) average cost weighting, (vi) publishing output weighting, (vii) importance of books over serials and (viii) local library use.*

Priority ranking of the subject are as and faculties has been suggested by Ehikhamenor[5]. The faculties which are started recently should get higher allotments in order to build an adequate core collection for them. Special attention has also to be given to there search materials of the established faculties. In order to minimize discrepencies, it is necessary to keep acquisition strictly to the priority ranking.

The optimal distribution of book funds among academic spartmerits is to be achieved first through allocating the lower required funds to all the departments. The remainder of the funds has to be allocated by selecting that department which attributed greater importance. This is to be determined the (i) social relevance of the subjects taught in the department, (ii) importance that the university gives to the work of the department and (iii) the importance due to the size of the department, enrollment, and faculty composition. Allocation of book is the basis of the above mentioned factor serves as ameans avoiding the monopoly of the funds by a few departments. Here, puts forth that the problem in book-fund allocation is to solved by applying the operational research technique or by the lower and upper limit of funds required for each department JS, Goyal[6] has given a normative prescription for distributing funds.

With regard to the allocation of funds to the acquisition I new materials, Arora[7] and Paul have recommended factors such

* The above mentioned variables have been adopted successfully in deciding the distribution of funds at Radford University.

(i) size of the library (ii) its goals and objectives, (iii) the characteristic of the library users - actual and potential and (iv) their information needs.

A simple test for the effectiveness of the allocation[8] is to correlate current buying or the distribution of books in the shelf list with circulations, using any non-parametric correlation statistic. If the correlations are high, the allocations are to be led as satisfactory; if low, the procedure needs re-examination.

This procedure is simple but pragmatic as it insists on demand based allocation.

The optimal distribution of the book-funds must be determined in the light of benefits and costs at the time when the decision is made i.e., the fund must be expended to the point where MBMC, for each department. Benefits from the library can be determined by the usage of the library materials. In other words, the efficient allocation of book-budget is achieved at the point where the difference between the total benefits and total cost is maximized. Thus, Gold[9] has suggested a logical procedure for measuring the economic efficiency by equating the Marginal benefits (output) and Marginal cost for each department.

Inflation is currently affecting library book budgets, particularly with respect to the acquisition of serials. To give allowance for this, MCG rath has advocated that besides library circulation data, average price of books in various subjects has to be taken into account due to the increase in the price level of monographs and serials.

According to Gold[10 11], distribution of book funds to various departments must take into consideration the inflationary the prices of books and periodicals in different subject as the rate of price inflation for each subject gets varied, case of a constant share of book fund to each department; there will be a relative reduction in the number of volumes acquired by departments whose price indexes rise more than average. In order to bring at an optimal allocation of book-funds, a larger share of the material funds has to be distributed to the department /subjects for which the rate of inflation is very high.

To balance the purchase of monographs and serials following factors are tobe taken in to consideration : (i) the number of funding units or the number of departments to which total book budget is to be apportioned and (ii) the percentage of monographs and serials required by each department.

Kohut[12] insists that balancing the acquisition of monographs with serials is an important factor to be considered as to maximise the potentiality of the university library to serve the information needs of the heterogeneous user groups. Koch[13] has recommended a budget model for book chasing in university libraries, taking in to account the rate which book prices increases each year; the increase in the number students and lecturers; and the number of multiple copies needed, in university has to establish a basic share for each department one point and allocate the following additional points per department:

(a) Lengthy course -1 point;
(b) others= 0.5 point;
(c) Unusually high priced books = 1 point;
(d) No. of academic and research staff or the number of students - 1 to 7.3 points.

These points are calculated for each departmental library according the nature of the department concerned, totalled and converteda percentage. According to the calculated percentages, the expenditure on monographs and periodicals is allocated.

It is clear from theabove studies that 'user strength' has been taken as an important determinant of allotment by Burton[1],

Goyal[6], Arora and Paul[7], Wei wood[7], Ehikhamenor[5], Koch[13] and Drake[2]. The number of academic and research departments have been suggested as abase for fund allotment by Kohut[12], Goyal[6], Wei wood[3], Ehikhamenor[5] and Drake[2]. The 'Cost of publication of books and periodical' are considered as vital factors by Burton[1], Gold[9], Kohut[12], Lewis[4] and Koch[13] while alloting the book fund by 'usage-based' allocation (utilisation) is recommended by Wei wood, Lewis[4] and MeGrath[8], An understanding of the 'requirement of monographs and serials' to the individual departments has been viewed as an essential factor by Kohut[12], Lewis[4] and Arora and Paul[7], while Ehikhamenor[5], Arora and Paul[7] and Burton[1] have considered the 'size of the existing collection' as an important variable for allocating the book-budget.

(ii) Effectiveness of Collection

The studies on collection evaluation have emphasized such criteria as (i) adequacy, (ii) effectiveness and (iii) efficiency. The adequacy has been measured in terms of (a) number of academic departments, (b) student population, (c) faculty composition and (d) researchers by Bonn[14], ACRL, Wilson[16], Clapp and Jordon[17], SCONUL, Down and Heusman[19], Ifidon[20], Stoljarov and Me Innis[22]. The utility of collection (circulation) has been suggested by Bonn[14], Wilson[25], Stoljarov[21] and Levine[27] to determine the effectiveness. The efficiency has been judged in terms of the least expensive book stock (unit cost) by Rowe[28].

To determine the adequacy of the collection for academic research, Bonnie has indicated the number of relevant volumes available per capita.

A ative criteria for adequacy of library[15] collections in academic libraries has been suggested by ACRL. It has stressed that each institution with 600 students should have atleast 50,000 volumes for every additional 200 students 10,000 volumes. This pinpoints the relationship between size of the library collection and the growth of the student population and expansion of academic programmes. To assess the adequacy of the collection size Wilson[16] has recommended a quantitative evaluation based on (i) users' need, (ii) external and (iii) internal standards.

Adequacy has also been expressed as a minimum size of library collection in institution of higher learning. In determining the minimum size, Clapp and Jordon[17] have taken into consideration such variables as the (i) size and characteristics of the student (ii) the size and research consciousness of the faculty, (iii) curriculum; i.e., the number of academic departments, (iv) fields of undergraduate 'majors' (v) fields of Master's and Doctor's degree, ect, (vi) methods of instruction, (vii) the intellectual climate of the university. He has suggested 42,000 volumes of books as the basic collection for an undergraduate library and prescribed additional 60 volumes per full time faculty member; 10 volumes for each enrolled student; 12 volumes for each honour's student; 240 volumes for each major undergraduate subject offered; 2400 volumes for every field in which Master's study is undertaken and 18000 volumes for every field in which study for Ph.D. is undertaken. From this, one can arrive at an indication of the minimum number of volumes required to support the academic programmes offered by the institution.

To Stoljarov, the optimum size of the library stock is to be determined by taking into account the number of volumes and 18000 volumes for every field in which study for Ph.D. is undertaken. From this, one can arrive at an indication of the minimum number of volumes required to support the academic programmes offered by the institution.

The Standing Conference of National and University Libraries (SCONUL)[18] has recommended thata university with 3000 undergraduates, 1000 research students and 500 teaching staff should posses a minimum of 500,000 volumes.

In there port for the Association of American College and Research Libraries, Downs and Heusman[19] have proposed that an average size of the stock for a university library should be two million volumes and 15,000 periodical titles with an annual acquisition rate of 100,000 volumes. This gives an average holding of 100 volumes and one current periodical title per student.

As against the prescription of minimum standards, Ifidon[20] has suggested a maximum number of books required by a library to support the academic programme of the parent institution. In deciding the maximum, the characteristic such as (i) a basic collection of 50,000 volumes for a university library whose parent institution has not less than four faculties, (ii) number of volumes per reader i.e. 30, (iii) the duration of an academic programme and the teaching staff members as a weighing factor (i.e. for one year's course etc.) and (iv) the required gross size of the book collection.

To Stoljarov[21], the optimum size of the library stock is to be determined by taking into account the number of volumes in stock and the number of readers. The author has remarked that any attempt to optimise the size of the stock must pay regard to the use per volume.

Me lnnis[22] has applied the regression analysis to find out the relationship between such variables as library holdings, current periodical titles, student enrollment, total number of doctoral fields and faculty members.

According to Bonn[23], utility of the collection is to be assessed by comparing the holding statistics with circulation statistics. Morse[24] has suggested that the active and inactive collection of a library can be easily assessed by taking into account the number of books borrowed and consulted in the library. Qualitative judgement is used to measure the capability of the collection[25] by Wilson. The criteria used in the evaluation of the collections are (i) circulation statistics, (ii) failure surveys,

(iii) standard lists and (iv) document delivery test. This evaluation indicates the strength and weaknesses of the collection in the various subject fields which lead to further improvement or remedial action.

To increase the utility of the library collection, Stoljarov[26] has suggested two ways viz., either by increasing the number of loans per reader or by decreasing the number of books per reader.

The productivity of the library holding can be assessed by taking into consideration the (a) circulation and (b) acquisition. Levine[27] has suggested that inorder to maximise the productivity, the acquisition should be made proportional to circulation. Rowe[28] has developed a micro-economic model to find out the least expensive stock by taking into consideration factors such as capital cost and operational cost.

(c) Evaluating the Performance of the Processing Unit

The studies on evaluation of the technical unit have taken into account cost factors and service factors. The studies by Fasana and Fall[1], Maier[2], Wessel[4], Tuttle[7], Misra and Phadke[6], Brutcher[8], Hayes and Becker[9], Leimkuhler and Cooper[10], Waldhart[5] and Marcum have considered such items as (i) personnel, (ii) raw materials (stationery) and (iii) overhead for the calculation of input cost or processing cost while (i) the number of volumes processed, and (ii) the total catalogue cards prepared for the computation of total output or production of the Technical unit.

For computing the cost of processing, Fasana[1] and Fall[1] have taken into consideration (i) the major activities of the processing unit, (ii) the types of personnel employed, (iii) the stationery used, (iv) the cost involved in carrying out the entire routine and (v) the number of cards produced.

The cost of technical services in academic libraries has been analysed by Maier[2]. To him, the cost factor includes labour cost, supply cost, overhead cost (equipment and furniture), transportation cost, binding cost and cost of processing per volume. The output measures of the technical unit include volumes added to the collection during a given period and added volumes processed.

The functioning of the technical unit can be measured in terms of their efficiency, economy and speed in contributing to the ability of the library to meet the needs of its present and potential users. The academic libraries are concerned not simply with providing the items available in the library but to see that the items are made available speedily.

Technical[3] services lend themselves more readily to precise measurement. To measure the efficiency and effectiveness of the operation of this unit, Wessel[4], Waldhart and Marcum[5] have taken into account the variables such as the personnel cost, the operational output (number of documents catalogued) and the marginal productivity[5].

For measuring the output of the technical unit, unit cost of technical processing has been taken as an important factor by Misra and Phadke[6]. According to them for measuring the performance, it is necessary to specify the nature and quantity of output. Once the units of output have been clearly defined, it can be related to the input cost. The input costs include the traditionally accepted expenses on labour, services and overheads, etc.

Tuttle[7] has suggested that the performance of the technical service can be evaluated by correlating the production of the technical unit with that of the cost involved in the total operation of this unit.

To calculate the total processing cost, Brutcher[8] has taken into account the labour cost involved in classification, cataloguing and physical preparations of the volumes; material and equipment cost. The unit cost has been calculated by considering the variables such as the (i) total technical processing cost and (ii) total volumes processed.

Hayes and Becker[9] have attempted to estimate cataloguing by taking into account salaries of the personnel employed in the technical section and the overhead expenses.

The standard costs based on the number of items processed the cost involved in processing has been recommended by Leimkuhler[10] and Cooperto[11] measure the performance of the technical unit.

(d) Evaluating the Performance of the Service Unit

Studies relating to the evaluation of the service-unit have taken in to consideration (i) cost items such as labour, building, and equipment and (ii) service items such as number of (a) documents circulated, (b) reference questions answered, (c) registered borrowers and (d) visitors. The studies of Hayes and Borko[1], Klintoe[2], Rowe[3], Lipetz[4], Martyn and Lancaster[5], and Standera[6] have attempted to measure the effectiveness of services by calculating the cost per item of output, while the studies by Van House[7], Evans et. al., Kantor and Deprospo, and Zweizig have taken into consideration only the output measures excluding the input.

Here, Hayes and Borko[1] have attempted to measure effectiveness of the library by taking the size of the library selection and labour as the capital investment and circulation the production. They have tried to bring out the correlation between these two variables.

Klinto[2] has presented the bre.k down of costs into libraries and materials for each of several services provided and a list of accomplishments for that service during the same period. So that the funding agent can see exactly how the alloted amount is spent on the various input items and assess the extent of benefit/use derived from it.

To identify the effectiveness of library services, Rowe[3] has introduced the concept of average cost of using the library. If the average cost of lending and reference transaction diminishes over the period of study, it is assumed that the library is used more frequently which, in turn, reflects the effectiveness of the service.

To determine the efficiency of the service unit, Lipetz[4] has taken into consideration the cost involved in materials, supplies, personnel and equipment; and also the products of the library operation which are useful to the patrons such as reference service, preparation of bibliographies and circulation. The efficiency ratio is taken as a guide line to judge the functioning of the service unit.

For measuring the quality of the services Martyn and Lancaster[5], and Standera[6] have recommended such criteria as (1) cost per loan transaction; (2) cost per user and (3) average cost per question answered.

As against this, van House has suggested such criteria as (i) circulation per capita, (ii) in-library materials use per capita, (iii) library visits per capita, (iv) reference transactions per capita, (v) registration as percentage of population and (vi) turn-over rate (circulation per volume).

Evans et al., Kantor,[9] De Prospo,[10] and Z'weizig[11] have suggested measures to evaluate level of performance of the service nit, which include (l) total circulation, (2) reference questions answered, (3) registered borrowers and (4) visitors. It is assumed that the level of performance increases in proportion to the increase in the number of services.

Notes

(a) General Performance Measures:

1. F.W. Lancaster and W.D. Climenson. "Evaluating the Economic Efficiency of a Document Retrieval system". Journal of Documentation, Vol. 24, No. 1: March 1968; pp. 16-25.

2. John J. Knightly. "Overcoming the criterion problem in the evaluation of library performance" Special Libraries. Vol.70, No. 4: April 1979; pp. 173-178.

3. Roderick M. Duchesne. "Analysis of Costs and Performance". Library Trends, April 1973; pp. 587-603.

4. D.H. Revill. "Availability as a performance measure for academic libraries". Journal of Librarianship, Vol. 19, No. l: January 1987; pp. 14-29.

5. Christine Oldman. "Demonstrating library value: a report of a research investigation". In: Anthony Vaughan (Ed.), Studies in Library Management, Vol. 7, London: Clive Bingley, 1982; pp. 117-143.

6. P.H. Sewell. "The evaluation of library services in depth". Unesco Bulletin for Libraries, Vol. 22: November-December 1968; pp. 274-280.

7. Stuart Hannubuss. "The concept of performance: a semantic review". Aslib Proceedings, Vol. 39, No. 5: 1987; pp. 149-158.

8. Morris Hamburg, Leonard E. Ramist and Michael R.W. Bommer. "Library objectives and Performance measures and their use in decision making". Library Quarterly, Vol. 42: 1972; pp. 107-123.

9. Janice Ladendorf. "Information service evaluation: The gap between the ideal and the possible". Special Libraries, Vol. 64, No. 7: July 1973; pp. 273-279.

10. Douglas L. Zweizig. "Measuring Library Use". Drexel Library Quarterly, Vol. 13, No. 3: July 1977; pp. 1-32.

11. Philip V. Rzasa and Norman R. Baker. "Measures of Effectiveness for a University Library". Journal of the American Society for Information Science, July-August 1972; pp. 248-253.

12. Vern M. Pings. "Development of Quantitative Assessment of Medical Libraries". College and Research Libraries, September 1968: pp. 373-381.

13. Rosemary Ruhig Du Mont and Paul R. Du Mont. "Measuring library effectiveness: a review and assessment". Advances in Librarianship, Vol. 9; 1979; pp. 104-141.

(b) Performance of the Acquisition Unit:

1. Robert E. Burton. "Formula Budgeting: An Example". Special Libraries, February 1975; pp. 61-67.

2. Miriam A. Drake. "Attribution of Library Costs". College and Research Libraries, November 1977; pp. 514-519.

3. R.J. Weiwood. "Book-Budget Allocation: An objective formula for the small academic library". Canadian Library Journal, Vol. 34, No. 3: 1977; pp. 213-219.

4. Lewis. "Bibliographic Materials Fund Allocation". Collection Development, Vol. 6, No. 3/4: Fall/Winter, 1984; pp. 37-47.

5. Fabian A. Ehikhamenor. "A Formula forAllocating Book Funds: The search for simplicity and flexibility". Libri, Vol. 33, No. 2: 1983; pp. 148-161.

6. S. K. Goyal. "Allocation of Library funds to different departments of a University: An Operational Research Approach". College and Research Libraries, May 1973; pp. 219-222.

7. Sant R. Arora and Rameshwar N. Paul. "Acquisition of Library Materials: A quantitative approach". In: American Society for Information Science, Proceedings, 6, San Francisco, Westport, Conn., and London: Greenwood, 1969; pp. 495-499.

8. William E. Me Grath. "A pragmatic Book Allocation Formula for Academic and Public Libraries: With a Test for its Effectiveness/Library Resources and Technical Services, Vol. 11, No. 4: Fall 1975; pp. 357-369.

9. Steven D. Gold. "Allocating the Book Budget: An Economic Model". College and Research Libraries, September 1975; pp. 397-402.

10. William E. Me Grath. Op. cit., pp. 357-369.

11. Steven D. Gold. Op. cit., pp. 397-402.

12. Joseph J. Kohut. "Allocating the Book-Budget: A model". College and Research Libraries, May 1974; pp. 192-218.

13. Hans-Albecht Koch."Research on budgeting and standard for academic libraries in the Federal Republic of Germany". Journal of Librarianship, Vol. 17, No. 4: October 1985; pp. 268-291.

14. George S. Bonn. "Evaluation of the collection". Library Trends, January 1974; pp. 265-303.

15. American Library Association, Association of College and Research Libraries, Draft: Standards for College Libraries, 1975 Revision, College and Research Libraries News, 11: November 1974; pp. 284-305.

Also in_ Sam E. Ifidon. "Establishment of Standards for Book stock in West African University Libraries". Libri, Vol. 33, No. 2: 1983; pp. 92-106.

16. T.D. Wilson. "The Evaluation of Bibliographical Resources".

In: F. W. Lancaster, and C. W. Cleverdon (Eds.), Evaluation and Scientific Management of Libraries and Information Centres, Noordhoff-Leyden, 1977; pp. 27-40.

17. V.W. Clapp and R.T. Jordan. "Quantitative criteria for Adequacy of Academic Library Collections". College and Research Libraries, Vol. 26, No. 5: September 1965; pp. 371-380.

18. Great Britain University Grants Committee, Committee on Libraries. Report, London: HMSO, 1967; pp. 264-281.

19. R.B. Downs and J.W. Heusman. "Standards for University Libraries". College and Research Libraries, Vol. 31, No. l: January 1970; pp. 28-35.

20. Sam E. Ifidon. "Establishment of Standards for Bookstock in West African University Libraries". Libri, Vol. 33, No. 2: 1983; pp. 92-106.

21. J.N. Stoljarov. "Optimum size of Public Library Stocks". Unesco Bulletin for Libraries, Vol. 7, No. l: Jan-Feb 1973; pp. 22-28.

22. R. Marvin Me Innis. "The formula approach to Library size: An empirical study of its efficacy in evaluating Research Libraries". College and Research Libraries, May 1972; pp. 190-198.

23. George S. Bonn. Op. cit., pp. 265-303.

24. P.M. Morse. "Measures of library effectiveness". Library Quarterly, Vol. 42: 1972; pp. 15-30.

25. T.D. Wilson. Op. cit., pp. 27-40.

26. J.N. Stoljarov. Op. cit., pp. 22-28.

27. M.M. Levine. "The circulation/Acquisition Ratio: An Input-output Measure for Libraries". Information Processing and Management, Vol. 16: 1980; pp. 313-318.

28. D. Rowe. "Application of the theory of the firm to library costing". Aslib Reader Series, Vol. 5: London: Aslib, 1984; pp. 301-305.

(c) Performance Measures of Technical Unit:

1. Paul J. Fasana and James E. Fall. "Processing costs for science monographs in the Columbia University Libraries". LRTS, Vol. 11, No. 1:.Winter 1967; pp. 97-114.

2. John M. Maier. "Analyzing Acquisitions and cataloguing costs", LRTS, Vol. 13, No. 1: Winter 1969; pp. 127-135.

3. Ahmed H. Helal."Approaches to the evaluation of Technical Services in Libraries". In: F.W. Lancaster and C.W. Cleverdon (Eds.), Evaluation and Scientific Management of Libraries and Information Centres, Noordh off-Leydon 1977; pp. 101-130.

4. C.J. Wessel. "Criteria for Evaluating Technical Library Effectiveness". Aslib Proceedings, Vol. 20, No. 11: 1968; pp.

5. Thomas J. Waidhart and Thomas P. Marcum."Productivity measurement in academic libraries. Advances in Librarians hip. Vol. 6: Newyork: Academic Press, 1976; pp. 54-75.

6. V.N.' Misra and D.N. Phadke. "Study on Unit costing of technical processing in an academic library". Papers presented at the XII IASLIC National Seminar, Varanasi, December 28-31, 1986; pp. 55-67.

7. Helen Welch Tuttle. "Standards for Technical Service Cost Studies". Advances in Librarianship, Vol. 1: 1970; pp. 95-111.

8. Constance Brutcher."Cost accounting for Library". LRTS, Vol. 8, No. 4: Fail 1964; pp. 413-417.

9. R.M. Hayes and J. Becker, "Cost accounting in libraries". In: Handbook of data processing for libraries. Newyork: Wiley/ Becker-Hayes, 1970; pp. 85-105.

10. Ferdinand F. Leimkuhler and Michael D. Cooper. "Cost accounting and analysis for University Libraries". College and Research Libraries, Vol. 36, No. 6: November 1971; pp. 449-464.

(d) Performance Measures of the Service Unit:

1. Robert M. Hayes and Harold Borko. "Mathematical models of information system use". Information Processing and Management, Vol.19, No. 3: 1983; pp. 187-190.

2. K. Klintoe. "Cost analysis of technical information Unit". Aslib Proceedings, Vol. 23, No. 7: July 1971; pp. 362-371.

3. D. Rowe. "Application of the theory of the firm to Library costing". In: Stephen A. Roberts (Ed.) Costing and the economics of library and information services. Aslib Reader Series, Vol. 5, London: Aslib, 1984; pp. 301-304.

4. Ben-Ami, Lipètz. "The Evaluation of communication systems: some Thoughts on Effectiveness". Science and Technology News, Winter 1966; pp. 110-113.

5. John Martyn and F.W. Lancaster. Investigative methods in library and information science: An introduction. Virginia: Information Resources Press, 1981; p. 182.

6. Oldrich R. Standera."Cost and effectiveness in the valuation of an information system: A case study". Journal of the American Society for Information Sciences, Vol. 25, No. 3: May-June 1974; pp. 203-207.

7. Nancy A. Van House. "Public Library Effectiveness: Theory, Measures and Determinants". LISR, Vol. 8: 1986; pp. 261-283.

8. Edward Evans, Harold Borko and Patricia Ferguson. "Review of criteria used to measure library effectiveness" In: Ross Shimmon (Ed.) A Reader in Library Management. London: Clive Bingley, 1976; pp. 166-180.

9. Paul B. Kantor. "Evaluation and Feedback". Annual Review of Library and Information Science, Vol. 4: 1981; pp. 100-120.

10. Ernest R. Deprospo. Performance measures for public Libraries. Chicago: ALA Public Library Association, 1973; p. 39.

11. Douglas L. Zweizig. "Measuring Library use". Drexel Library Quarterly, Vol. 13, No. 3: July 1977; pp. 1-32.

3

Research Design

Higher education in India has witnessed a period of prosperity and growth since Independence. In order to make it more purposeful and socially relevant, changes have been made in the National educational policy. Recently, research has been given added emphasis, and the Universities are becoming more of research-oriented centres rather than mere teaching institutions. In this context, the University Libraries have been vested with the responsibility of making available to the users not only adequate resources but also a large number of bibliographic tools and services. But in the process of fulfilling the new role assumed by the Universities, their Libraries confront a number of challenging situations.* The phenomenal increase in the number of students at the graduate, postgraduate and research levels, the proliferation of new subject areas, the growth in the number of books published and the extensive

---

* This situation is common to almost all the University Libraries in India.

expansion of library materials are some of the factors to be reckoned with in the organization and functioning of University Libraries. Further more, the spiralling of the material, labour and overhead costs, growing library expenditure, and the limited additional investment made on the libraries are the other factors which demand a deeper analysis of the potentiality of the libraries to fulfil the tasks.* There is also an increasing pressure upon the library staff to maintain the standards of the library services at a satisfactory level with in the available infrastructure. This situation calls for an examination of the functioning and performance of the University libraries, their problems and prospects in order (i) to identify the strengths and weaknesses of the operations of the University libraries; (ii) to find out the ways and means of solving those problems; and (iii) suggest remedial measures.

(a) Objectives

In the light of the above situation, the following objectives are framed for this research study to ensure the application of scientific research methods to the examination of the issues involved.

1. To examine the trend in the growth of library finance.

2. To analyse the pattern of its allocations among the input items.

3. To assess the adequacy and efficiency of the library resources.

4. To identify the level of performance of the library units such as (i) Acquisition Unit, (ii) Processing Unit and (iii) Service Unit.

---

* Among the major obstacles to University Library development the following seem to stand out promptly: (i) inadequate financial support; (ii) inadequate physical facilities (iii) failure to appoint competent staff etc.

Source: M.A. Gelfand. University Libraries for developing Countries. Delhi: Universal Book Co., 1974. p. 14.

5. To measure the over-all performance of the Library in terms of Cost-effectiveness analysis.

In recent years, the University Library finances are at a low ebb and progress in the availability of finances for the expansion of library facilities is tardy if not inadequate. Hence, it will be appropriate to examine the trends in the growth of library finances.

The allocation of funds among the input items such as library materials, manpower and other physical facilities is not planned properly and carried out scientif ically, and it is reflected in the mis-match between the availability of various categories of library materials and services and their respective demands by the users. This situation warrants an investigation of the allocational pattern of the University libraries.

The procedures* adopted for developing the library collections are not appropriate to fulfil the information requirements of the users. The Acquisition Unit is not able to achieve its objective of making available the relevant literature due to the delay in the selection of books and periodicals; belated ordering and payment; and above all the inadequate and improper allocation of funds. This situation requires a deeper analysis to find out the problems in the existing practices in the Acquisition Unit so as to suggest alternatives which will improve the performances. Lack of adequate, qualified and competent staff members is another major issue which used to affect the efficiency of the Library services. Hence an analysis of the volume of work done by the Technical and Service Units is an absolute necessity in order to understand the present level of performance of these Units and to find out methods that will increase the outputs. Besides, the efforts made in the direction of evaluating the total performance of the libraries are limited

---

* The procedures here refers to the book-budget allocation and the book-selection policies.

in the Indian Universities and hence there exists no sound perspectives with regard to maximizing the output with the given input. Keeping in view of the above mentioned factors, the present study is undertaken.

(b) Methodology

(i) Data Collection Primary

This study involves collection of secondary data to be gathered from the records of the Libraries of the two Universities concerned, taken up for study, on the following aspects:

1. The data pertaining to the financial allotment of the library have been collected from Budget Estimates of the sample University Libraries.

2. Information regarding the number of books and periodicals and their relative cost have been gathered from Accession and Periodical Registers.

3. Data on the number of Library staff and their salaries have been collected from their respective Service Registers.

4. Information regarding the total area of the Library buildings and their costs have been collected from the Records of the Work Section.

5. Data on the total number of furniture and their cost have been gathered from the Maintenance Records of the Library.

6. Information regarding the total number of books added, processed and circulated have been collected from the Annual Reports of the University; total number of circulation by subjects have been taken from the circulation Records maintained by the Library.

7. Data on the total number of departments, details of the courses offered, number of students enrolled, number of scholars registered, and the staff strength have been taken from Annual.

Reports.*

(ii) Statistical Tools

To carry out the objectives of the study, the following statistical tools, have been employed.

1. *'t' - test*: To test the changes in the financial provision of the University Library over the years, the non-parametric 't' test has been adopted.

2. *Multiple Regression Model*: To measure the combined effect of variables such as new books added, total working hours and the number of volumes processed on the Unitcostof Processing, a multiple regression model has been adopted.

3. *Simple Linear Regression Model*: To estimate the influence of books processed on circulation a simple linear regression model is used.

4. *Benefit-cost Ratio*: To measure the Benefit-cost Ratio (BCR) of the Service Unit, the marginal analysis of the cost and services have been attempted.

5. *Log-Linear regression model*: To analyse the factors influencing the circulation of the library, the log-linear regression model has been adopted.

(c) Concepts Library Finance

Library Finance indicates the grants received by each library from the various funding agencies in order to run the

* However, a limited and specific survey of the users' opinion is conducted with a view to testing the soundness of the proposition and conclusions of the study.

library efficiently. The primary sources of funds to the libraries are collected from agencies such as University Authorities and University Grants Commission. Others include (i) endowment grants received from the Ford Foundation, Rockfeller Foundation and the Public Law 480 funds; (ii) adhoc grants from the national and international organisations; (iii) fees and fines.

Allocation

Allocation is the process of deciding what proportion of the library finance is to be assigned to the various library-units or expenditure categories. The manner in which the libraries accomplish their fund allocation varies widely according to the fund availability, academic climate of the University and the demand of the user community.

Input Items

1. Input items refer to the library materials, personnel, space and overhead connected with each functional unit of the library viz: (i) Acquisition Unit, (ii) Processing Unit and (iii) Service Unit.

Adequacy of the Library Resources

It implies a quantitative criteria used for measuring the financial provision and collection development based on the requirements. Requirement is to be decided on the basis of the user population.

Efficiency of the Library Resources

It is a qualitative criteria used to assess at one level the rational distribution of the finance among the input items in the order of their contribution to the library performance; and at another level it implies the relevant and useable collection.

(d) Limitations

(1) This study is related to only two of the ten University Libraries functioning in Tamil Nadu. The Madras University Library has been left out, as it is more than

100 years old, and it is not comparable with the other younger Universities in the State. The Libraries of the Alagappa University, the Anna University.

The Tamil Nadu Agricultural University, the Tamil University and the Mother Teresa Women's University have been left out as they are of very recent origin and are less than twelve years old and they are also not comparable to the Annamalai University and Madurai Kamaraj University. These two University Libraries have alone been chosen for the purpose as they are more than twenty years old and much enlightenment can be had by comparing their respective performances.

(2) This study is restricted to three major Units of each of the Library viz: (i) Acquisition Unit, (ii) Processing Unit and (iii) Service Unit excluding the Reprography and Documentation as they are not in fulfledged operation in the sample University Libraries.

(3) The period of study is limited to twenty years from 1967 to 1987.*

---

* Since the Madurai Kamaraj University Library which was established in 1967 has completed 20 years of its existence in 1987, this duration has been chosen for the present study.

4

Profile of the Sample University Libraries

The system of higher education in Tamil Nadu has been flourishing since1960's due tothe establishment of a large number of academic and research institutions. Incentives to the higher learning has been given by instituting a number of academic and research libraries at various levels. Taking the Universities alone, there are 10 University Libraries in Tamil Nadu. Based on the type of Universities in which the Libraries are functioning, they are broadly classified as Libraries belonging to the (i) Affillating type of Universites, (ii) Unitary type of Universities, (iii) Agricultural Universities, (iv) Technical Universities and (v) "Deemed to be Universities".

Among the existing libraries, (i) Madras University Library (1857), (ii) Madurai Kamaraj University Library (1966), (iii) Bharathiar University Library (1982), (iv) Bharathidasan University Library (1982) and (v) Mother Teresa University Library (1984) belong to the first category; (i) Annamalai University Library (1929), (ii) Tamil University Library (1981) and (iii) Alagappa University Library (1985) belong to the second category; Tamil Nadu Agricultural University Library (1971) belongs to the third; Anna University Library (1978) belongs to the fourth and Gandhigram Rural Institute Library (1976) belongs to the fifth categories. Based on the year of establishment,these Libraries can be brought under two heads viz: (i) Libraries established before Independence and (ii) after Independence. Except the Madras and Annamalai University Libraries, the others have been formed only during the last two decades. The sample libraries for the present study has been chosen by taking into account such factors as (i) nature/type of the library viz: (a) affiliated or (b) Unitary and (ii) the year of establishment viz: (a) before Independence and (b) after Independence. The Annamalai University Library has been selected on the basis of Unitary type of library, established before Independence and the Madurai Kamaraj University Library has been taken on the basis of Affiliated type of library, established after Independence.

Annamalai University Library

The Annamalai University Library was established in 1927 by the founder father Sir Annamalai Chettiar in order to support the growing academic and research programmes of the University. Apart from the Main Library situated at the heart of the University, 44 Departmental Libraries have been functioning in the various departments of the University. In addition, a study centre has been instituted for the benefit of the under-graduates.

The Main Library located at the centre of the campus occupies a built-in-area of about 3,600 square feet. For the convenient functioning of the Library, the Administrative sections viz: (i) the Acquisition and (ii) the Technical sections have been placed in the West wing of the Library and the Service Unit occupies a larger area of the Library. The UGC has granted a sum of Rs. 11.5 lakhs for the construction of the building and Rs. 4.3 lakhs for the purchase of equipment and furniture.

The major sources of finance to the AUL are the University funds and UGC grants. It has received a sum of Rs. 175.14 lakhs upto December 1987. An annual average of Rs. 8.3 lakhs has been sanctioned to this library, out of which Rs. 8.1 lakhs has been spent for recurring items such as books, periodicals and personnel and Rs. 0.2 lakhs for non-recurring items such as building, furniture and equipments.

The total collection of AUL has crossed 3 lakhs (Books: 273790; periodicals: 34391). The library adds annually 11507 Books and 1245 periodicals. The sixth edition of Colon classification has been used for the purpose of classification and 5th edition of the classified catalogue code has been used for preparing the catalogue cards. The new titles received are listed periodically and sent to the respective Departments in order to keep them aware of the new books acquired in their subject concerned. The processed books are transferred to the stock-room regularly for the display. In view of safety measures, closed access has been adopted. The Library remains open on all the days of a year. The circulation section functions from 10 A.M. to 5 P.M. The total number of registered borrowers are about 8900 and nearly 320 books have been issued on an average per day.

The total number of staff members of the AUL are 33. The Acquisition Unit consists of 3 professionals, 4 LDC and non-professionals; the Technical Unit consists of 3 qualified technical staff members, LDC, 2 Binders and 4 non-professionals; and the Service Unit consists of 2 Library Assistants, LDC and 3 non-professionals. AUL is catering to the information needs of 1350 under-graduates, 800 post-graduates, 270 researchers, and 550 staff members on an average every year.

Madurai Kamaraj University Library

The Madurai Kamaraj University Library (MKUL) was established in the year 1966 under the stewardship of Dr. T.P. Meenakshi Sundaram, the first Vice-Chancellor of the University. In addition to the Central Library, there are about

17 Departmental Libraries,* and one Evening College Library. Besides, three study centres have been established at Madurai, Palayamkottai and Nager coil for the benefit of the students of the various colleges affiliated to the Madurai Kamaraj University.

The Library is situated at the centre of the University Campus. It accommodates a carpet area of 3200 square feet.

A sum of Rs. 11 lakhs has been spent on the construction of the Library Building. The entire Library Building has a seating capacity for 650 readers at a time and a stacking capacity to accommodate 2 lakhs of books. The library has build-in spaces for all the essential facilities such as (i) separate reading rooms for books and periodicals, (ii) carrels for research scholars, (iii) exhibition hall, (iv) staff reading room etc. The MKUL is furnished with modern equipments and furniture worth of Rs. 2.71 lakhs.

MKUL is getting grants mainly from the (i) University Budget and (ii) UGC, for the recurring and non-recurring items of expenditure. It has received a sum of Rs. 27.3 lakhs upto December 1987. An annual average grant of Rs. 11.8 lakhs has been alloted to the library, out of which Rs.11.55 lakhs (97.9%) has been spent for the purchase of books and periodicals and payment of the staff salaries etc.; and the remaining 0.3 lakhs (2.1%) has been spent for the building, furniture and equipments.

For the purpose of efficient functioning, the library has been organised into various sections such as (i) Acquisition,

---

* The Departmental Libraries have been established in Departments such as, (i) Biology, (ii) Chemistry, (iii) Physics, (iv) Mathematics, (v) Economics, (vi) Education, (vii) Library Science, (viii) Sociology, (ix) History, (x) Poiitical Science, (xi) Management, (xii) Commerce, (xiii) English, (xiv) Linguistics, (xv) Gandhian Thought, (xvi) Dravidian and Foreign Languages and (xvii) Thirukkural Chair.

(ii) Technical and (iii) Service. It has acquired 2.05 lakhs of books and 11075 periodicals. MKUL adds annually 1059 books and 634 periodicals to its collection. In addition to the current subscriptions, back volumes of journals have also been acquired in different subjects. The number of volumes processed amounts to 2.1 lakhs. For the purpose of classification, the third edition of colon classification is used, and a classified catalogue on card is available in the Library. Ready-for-use books are displayed in the 'New Arrival' corner for wider publicity. All the processed books are put on the open shelves for easy access without any formality or hindrance between the readers and the books. The circulation section has been working from 8 A.M. to 8 P.M. The total number of registered borrowers on 1st December was nearly 5500 and 290 books have been issued on an average per day. It is equipped with general and subject reference collections, of all kinds such as encyclopaedias, handbooks, biographies, bibliographies, atlases, gazetteers, statistical tables, annuals and directories.

The staff strength of MKUL amounts to 34, out of which 13 are qualified personnel, 14 clerical staff, 1 Binder and 9 non-professionals. From the existing staff, 3 professionals, 4 clerks and 3 non-professionals have been employed in the Acquisition Unit; 6 Technical staff members, 4 clerks, 1 Binder and 3 non-professionals have been posted in the Technical Unit and the remaining 4 Senior Technical staff, 4 clerical staff and 3 non-professionals have been appointed in the Service Unit.

5

A Comparative Analysis of the Finances of the Libraries of the Annamalai University and the Madurai Kamaraj University

The success of the library activities in any University mainly revolves around such factors as (i) accumulation and dissemination of relevant information and (ii) designing the requirements of the academic programme of the University. This, in turn, depends upon the (i) adequate provision of finance to the library and (ii) its judicious expenditure which will maximise the effectiveness of the library activities.

The financial requirements of the University libraries are of two types: (i) recurring and (ii) non-recurring. The recurring funds are needed to pay for the items such as (i) staff salaries, (ii) book acquisition, (iii) periodical subscription, (iv) stationery, (v) maintenance and replacement of furniture and fittings. The non-recurring grants are required for the buildings, furniture and equipment. The quantum of allotment for both the items (recurring and non-recurring) depends to a large extent, on the age of the University library.* The continuous and steady flow of recurring and non-recurring funds will enable the libraries to maintain the standards and enhance the effectiveness of library services.

But in reality, libraries function within limited financial resources and have constraints in framing their budgets. Hence the available funds have to be allocated efficiently, by taking into account the following factors: (i) the academic programmes of the University, (ii) the total user population, (iii) the existing sources and availability of funds, (iv) the material, manpower and other physical facilities required to support the academic activities and (v) the future requirements. This will ensure the overall efficient performance of the library services.

Against this background, the following aspects have been taken up for analysis in respect of the sample University Libraries for the period 1967-1987: (i) trends in the financial provision and its adequacy and (ii) the pattern of allocation of funds and its efficiency.

Trends in the Financial Provision of the AUL and MKUL

The sources of funds available to the University Library are from (i) University Budget allocation, (ii) grants from the University Grants Commission and others. The University allocation refers to that portion of the total University finances which is alloted to the library. This consists of the (a) funds alloted by the State Government to the University and (b) the Library fees collected along with the tuition fees from the

---

* For instance, the older Universities require more of recurring funds, since they have larger academic programmes and consequently they have to serve a larger user population. On the other hand, new Universities require huge non-recurring grants as they have to start everything from the scratch, i.e., the constructions of buildings, purchase of equipment and furniture.

Table 1
Trends in the Financial Provision of AUL and MKUL (Rupees in Lakhs)

	Annamalai University Library			*Madurai Kamaraj University Library*			
Plan period	*Total financial provision (during the plan)*	*Annual average provision*	*Growthrate over the previous plan period*	*Total financial provision (during the plan)*	*Annual average provision*	*Growthrate over the previous plan period*	*between the two total financial provision*
A	6.58	2.2	100	8.3	2.8	100	3:4
IV	17.25	3.4	265	28.0	5.6	337	1:2
V	30.69	6.1	472	42.0	8.4	506	3:4
VI	68. 19	13.6	1048	88.4	17.7	1065	2:3
VI I	52.43	17.5	806	80.6	26.9	971	2:3
Total	175.14	8.3		247.3	11.8		2:3

Source: Computed

students and research scholars. Funds from University Grants Commission are given for each five-year plan period not only for books and periodicals but also for building, equipment and other infrastructure for the Library. Others include specific grants like Overseas Development Aid Programme, Wheat Loan Programme and also the fines collected. The adequacy of the library finance is to be tested in terms of (i) the growing volume of academic activities of the Universities, (ii) the student strength in the various courses, (iii) users' demand for library materils and services and (iv) the proportion of University finances alloted to the Library.

The total finance provided to AUL and MKUL over the years are presented in Table 1.

It is striking to note that the total financial provision inclusive of the UGC grants, University fund and other adhoc grants to AUL and MKUL has recorded an eleven fold increase. The funds received by the AUL has increased from Rs. 6.5 lakhs in the Annual plan period to Rs. 68.1 lakhs in the VI plan period, while that of MKUL from Rs. 8.13 lakhs to Rs. 88.4 lakhs. Over the plan period under review the total finance provided to the AUL amounts to Rs. 176 lakhs, while that of MKUL is Rs. 247 lakhs. Thus the financial provision of the MKUL has been higher than that of AUL in all the plan periods.

The annual average finance alloted to the AUL has increased from Rs. 2.2 lakhs to Rs. 17.5 lakhs during the study period while that of MKUL has increased from Rs. 2.8 lakhs to Rs. 26.9 lakhs. The highest amount has been alloted to the sample libraries only in the last two plan periods* The annual average for the whole period works out to be Rs. 8.3 lakhs in AUL and Rs. 11.8 lakhs for MKUL. The above analysis also has exhibited the marked differences among the Universities in the

* It is only during the VI and VII plan periods that the annual average has exceeded the total average.

provision of finance at every plan periods and the proportion of variation ranges from 27 points to 64 points.

An idea of the magnitude of the funds received by both the libraries can be had from Table 1. The ratio was 3:4 in the Annual and Fifth plan periods, while it was higher at 2:3 in the VI and VII plan periods. It was as much as 1:2 during the IV plan. This clearly indicates that the total finance received by the MKUL has always been higher than that of AUL. This may be attributed to the fact that MKUL being a new University Library has received more funds than the established University Libraries to organise and stabilise its services. An analysis of the sources and quantum of funds received by the Universities for the libraries may explain this trend.

Sources of Finance for the Sample Libraries

The main sources of finance to the University Libraries are from the (i) University Budget and (ii) UGC Grants. Adhoc and special grants are also received from the national organizations and international programmes. Data relating to the sources of finance to the sample libraries are given in Table 2.

It is striking to note from the table that the Budgetary provision of AUL has increased from Rs. 3.9 lakhs to Rs. 29.7 lakhs marking a 7.6 fold increase while that of MKUL has increased from Rs. 4.7 lakhs to Rs. 57.7 lakhs, recording a 12.3 fold increase. Thus the Budget Provision of MKUL has not only been higher than that of AUL in absolute terms, but the rate of increase in relative terms has also been significantly higher. This may be due to the fact that MKUL being a Government institution is getting greater allotment from the State Government. As a result University funds as percentage to total expenditure has shown a falling trend in AUL while MKUL has exhibited a rising trend. In the case of AUL, the University funds which was 59 percent in the Annual Plan period has touched the lowest level of 40 percent in the VI Plan period. As

Table 2A

Sources of Finance to AUL and MKUL (Rupees)

	Annamalai University				Madurai Kamaraj University Library			
Plan period	*University allocation*	*UGC grants*	*Other sources*	*Total*	*University allocation*	*UGC grants*	*Other sources*	*Total*
A	390700	250000	17680	658350	470200	362860	-	833060
	(59.3)	(38.0)	(2.7)	(100)	(56.4)	(43.6)		(100)
IV	71+9000	904200	72010	1725210	1353000	{WQ000	500i5	2803015
	(43.5)	(52.4)	(4.1)	(100)	(48.3)	(50.0)	(1.7)	(100)
V	1489000	156510	1500	3069100	2574300	160&000	22355	4204655
	(48.5)	0 (51.0)	(0.5)	(100)	(61.2)	(38.2)	(0.6)	(100)
VI	2771000	394900	99240	6819240	5898400	2900000	45150	8843550
	(40.6)	0 (57.0)	(1.5)	(100)	(66.7)	(32.8)	(0.5)	(100)
VII	2972000	220000	71120	5243120	5777000	2200000	85400	8062400
	(26.7)	0 (42.0)	(1.3)	(100)	(71.7)	(27.3)	(1.0)	(100)
Total	18371700	886830	275040	17515050	16072900	U70Z60	202920	24746680
	(47.8)	0 (50.6)	(1.6)	(100)	(65.0)	(34.0)	(1.0)	(100)

Source: Computed

against this, University funds of MKUL has started from 56 per cent and touched the peak of 72 percent. This is reflected in the average for the plan periods which works out to be 47.8 per cent for AUL and 65 per cent for MKUL. This confirms the hypothesis that MKUL being a new institution is getting greater allotment from the State Government than AUL which is a Unitary and Private Institution.

The UGC grants for AUL has increased from Rs. 2.5 lakhs to Rs. 39.5 lakhs recording a 15.8 fold increase while that of MKUL from Rs. 3.6 lakhs to Rs. 29 lakhs registering an 8 fold increase. Table 2 reveals that the grants of the UGC has shown a rising trend in AUL and falling trend in MKUL during the study period. In the case of AUL, the proportion of UGC grant which was 38 per cent of the total finances during the Annual Plan periods reached the peak of 42 per cent in the VII Plan periods. As against this, the proportion of UGC grant in MKUL which was 43.6 per cent at the initial stage gradually declined to 27.3 per cent in relative terms. But in absolute terms UGC grants have been higher upto the V Plan for the MKUL. The larger amount of UGC funds for AUL in the VI Plan is to support the introduction of new job-oriented and professional courses. But when the total amount of UGC grants received over the period is taken into account, it is found that both the universities have received more or less the same amount.

Other sources exhibit rather a mixed trend. AUL has received a total of Rs. 27 lakhs over the period, while that of MKUL Rs. 20 lakhs. This is attributed to the larger amount of library fees received by the AUL which is having a greater number of user population. In addition to this, AUL has also received sizeable specific grants from national organisations such as ICAR, and International Programmes such as ODA, and Wheat Loan Programmes. It is thus clear that among the sources of revenue, MKUL, has received larger amount of University Funds both in absolute and relative terms than that of AUL. In

Table 2B
Growth Rate of Finance to AUL and MKUL

Plan period	*Annamalai University Library*				*Madurai Kamaraj University Library*			
	University Allocation	*UGC grants*	*Other sources*	*Total*	*University Allocation*	*UGC grants*	*Other sources*	*Total*
A	100	100	100	100	100	100		100
IV	192	362	407	262	288	386	100	336
V	331	626	85	466	547	443	45	*505*
VI	709	1580	561	1036	1254	799	90	1062
VII	761	S80	402	796	1229	606	171	968

Source: Computed.

the case of UGC grants, both the Universities have obtained more or less the same amount.

Regarding other sources of revenue are concerned, AUL has received relatively larger amount than that of MKUL. An analysis of trends in the growth of these sources will give further insight into the position. The relevant data are given in Table 2B.

The trend in the growth of the finances of the AUL indicates that University funds for AUL has increased by 7.61 times, while that of MKUL by 12.1 times. But the rate of increase in the successive plan periods in both the institutions is the same viz. two times. As against this the rate of growth of UGC funds is gradual upto V Plan period in AUL and MKUL, but steeped in the VI Plan, which may perhaps be attributed to the human resource development programme initiated by the Government. It is interesting to note that the rate of growth of UGC grant in AUL exceeds the total growth rate of all sources while it is far below the total growth rate in MKUL. The larger provision of UGC funds to AUL during the sixth plan period is attributed to the starting of new courses in the Faculty of Arts and Sciences.

Table 3
Ratio of Financial Provision

Plan Period	*Ratio of University allocation in AUL and MKUL*	*Ratio of UGC funds in AUL and MKUL*	*Ratio of other sources of finance in AUL and MKUL*
A	1:1	1:1	-
IV	1:2	1:2	1:1
V	1:2	1:1	1:2
VI	1:2	2:1	2:1
VII	1:2	1:1	1:1
Total	1:2	1:1	1:1

An analysis of the different sources of finance of the sample libraries will make the point clear. This is attempted below. The ratio analysis given in Table 3 clearly indicates that barring the Annual plan periods, the ratio of University allocation in AUL and MKUL has been 1:2 in all the plan periods. This brings to light the fact that the University Funds received by the MKUL has been two times greater than that of AUL. In the Case of UGC Funds, except in the VI plan, in all other periods, the ratio is the same.

To test the changes in the financial provision of the sample Libraries over the years, the non-parametric 't' test has been adopted. It has been proceeded by formulating the null hypothesis that the provision of finance for both the libraries are the same. The difference between the totals of the two libraries (di) for each year has been calculated which became the value of a new variable D, which is equal to zero, i.e. E(D) MD=O.

For the given data $\overline{d}$ and $\hat{s}$ d have been calculated in the following manner as,

$\overline{d}$ = di/n, where n is the total number of years.

$$\hat{s}\,\mathrm{d} = \frac{\sqrt{n\Sigma di^2 - (\Sigma di)^2}}{n(n-1)} \quad \text{or} \quad \frac{\sigma n - 1}{\sqrt{n}}$$

with $\hat{s}$ d, the estimator of the standard error of $\overline{d}$ becomes $\hat{\sigma}$ d= $\hat{s}d / \sqrt{n}$. Finally, the ratio of to its standard error has been calculated by adopting d, which is used as the test statistic in this case.

Hypothesis:

$*H_0$: M_1 M_2

H_1 : M_1 M_2

Levels of significance : 0.01

Test statistic : d, which is distributed as tn-1

Decision Rule : Since n = 21 we have p (t20 > 2.845) = 0

H_Q will be rejected if and only if t20, >2.845. The results are given below:

t calculated value - 5.45

t tabulated value= 2.845 at 1% level

Since the computed 't' value is greater than the tabulated value, the Ho is rejected indicating that the total financial provision of AUL and MKUL is not the same. In other words, the 't' value for the difference between total finance is 5.45 which is highly significant. Hence, we conclude that the total library finance is not the same in both the universities. It is higher for MKUL.

In order to determine the range of difference, the confidence interval for the total financial provision is also computed. The calculation is as follows:

d^ (t tab) x (s d)

= 164 to 524

The range of difference between the total finance of MKUL and AUL will be between 164 to 524. In order to decide the source of finance that has caused the difference inthe total of MKUL, the 't' test has been applied for the UGC grants. Since the computed 't' value is lesser than the tabulated value (0.4747 < 2.845), it may be inferred that the UGC grants are the same for both the University libraries.

---

* H_Q = Total Library Finance of AUL & MKUL is the same.

It is thus clear from the above, that the difference in the total finance of MKUL is mainly due to the difference in the university allocation. The causes for this may be identified when we attempt a categorywise analysis of the funds as recurring and non-recurring. Among these two, recurring grants are more important as they are needed for staff salaries, book acquisition, subscription to periodicals, stationery and the repair of furniture and fitting. Non-recurring grants on the other hand, are required for the building, furniture and equipments.

The recurring and non-recurring grants received by the sample libraries have been presented in Table 4.

It is striking to note that the recurring grant for the AUL has recorded a 9 fold increase from Rs. 5.8 lakhs to Rs. 52.7 lakhs while that of MKUL has registered nearly, a 10 fold increase from Rs. 7.5 lakhs to Rs. 80 lakhs. In absolute terms, recurring grants have almost double din both the University Libraries during the successive plans. During the VI plan, it has touched the peak of Rs. 67 lakhs in AUL and Rs. 87 lakhs in MKUL. The total recurring grant during the period under review works out to be Rs. 171.6 lakhs in AUL while it is Rs. 242.5 lakhs in MKUL. Thus MKUL has received Rs. 71 lakhs more than that of AUL.

The Annual plan average of the recurring grants of AUL has ranged from Rs. 2 lakhs in the Annual plan period to Rs. 17.6 lakhs in the VII plan; while that of MKUL has ranged from Rs. 2.5 lakhs to Rs. 26.7 lakhs. The annual average of AUL is calculated as Rs. 8.2 lakhs and that of MKUL is Rs. 11.5 lakhs. The causes for this inequity is mainly due to the variation in the receipt of finance.

It is against this view point that the trends in non-recurring grants of the sample libraries have to be examined. The non-recurring grants of AUL has declined gradually from

Table 4

Annual Average Recurring and Non-Recurring Grants of AUL and MKUL (Rupees)

Plan Period	*Annamalai University Library*		*Madurai Kamaraj University Library*	
	Recurring Grants	*Non-recurring Grants*	*Recurring Grants*	*Non-recurring Grants*
A	195018 (100)	24442 (100)	249533 (100)	28153 (100)
IV	322492 (276)	22550 (154)	534577 (357)	26625 (154)
V	593440 (507)	20380 (139)	817394 (564)	23537 (139)
VI	1345433 (1150)	18415 (126)	1747470 (1162)	21240 (126)
VII	1757390 (901)	16983 (69)	2667866 (1069)	19600 (70)
Total	817336	20524	1154734	23680

Source : Computed.

Table 5
Analysis of Recurring Expenditure (Rupees)

Plan Period	*Annamalai University Library*				*Madurai Kamaraj University Library*			
	Books and Periodical expenditure	*Staff salaries*	*Miscella-neous*	*Total recurring expenditure*	*Books and periodical expenditure*	*Staff salaries*	*Miscella-neous*	*Total Recurring Expenditure*
A	411041 (70.2)	143940 (24.6)	30075 (5.2)	585055 (100)	525800 (70.2)	201060 (26.9)	21740 (2.6)	748600 (100)
IV	1189900 (73.8)	346969 (21.5)	75600 (4.7)	1612460 (100)	2004700 (75.0)	590580 (22.1)	77530 (2.8)	2672885 (100)
V	2264600 (76.3)	593700 (20.0)	108900 (3.7)	2967200 (100)	2956920 (72.3)	980680 (24.8)	150030 (3.6)	4086970 (100)
VI	5439275 (80.9)	1138740 (16.9)	149150 (2.2)	6727165 (100)	6926200 (79.3)	1559200 (17.8)	251940 (2.8)	8737350 (100)
VII	440800 (76.6)	1125620 (21.4)	105750 (2.2)	5272170 (100)	6425600 (803)	1393500 (17.4)	184410 (2.3)	8003600 (100)
Total	13345415 (77.8)	3348960 (19.5)	469475 (2.7)	17164050 (100)	18839220 (77.7)	4724540 (19.5)	685730 (2.8)	24249410 (100)

Source : Computed.

Rs. 0.7 lakhs to Rs. 0.5 lakhs, while that of MKUL has declined from Rs. 0.8 lakhs to Rs. 0.6 lakhs. During the successive plan periods, the non-recurring grants have shown a falling trend in both the Libraries* The total works out to be Rs. 4.3 lakhs in AUL and Rs. 5 lakhs in MKUL during the period under study.

The annual plan average of non-recurring grants of AUL have ranged from Rs. 0.2 lakhs to Rs. 0.16 lakhs, while that of MKUL from Rs. 0.3 lakhs to Rs. 0.19 lakhs. Over the years the annual average non-recurring grants is Rs. 0.2 lakhs in AUL and Rs. 0.24 lakhs in MKUL. Thus, the non-recurring grants for both the Libraries are the same. This again confirms the fact that the inequality in the finance is mainly due to the recurring expenditure, which is as it should be. The recurring expenditure of MKUL has been higher in absolute terms over the plan periods and it is higher than AUL by 41 percent.

Analysis of Recurring Expenditure

Recurring expenditure in the sample libraries may be broadly classified into three groups. The principal item among these groups is books and periodicals. The next item is staff salaries. This includes salaries of the professional and non-professional staff members. The third item miscellaneous incorporates stationery, binding, postage and contingency.

Of these three items, books and periodicals are predominant accounting for nearly three-fourths of the total

* FN: This is due to the law of indivisibility. Because of the indivisible nature of the items like building, furniture and equipment, they have to be erected and installed in one instalment. But as time passes by their cost spreads over the period of time and the cost per unit of time goes on decreasing. So it is in concurrence with the natural law of economics, viz., the law of indivisibility, inferring that the non-recurring items form lower percentage of total expenditure in Senior University libraries, and higher percentage in junior university libraries.

recurring expenditure. The staff salary accounts for only one-fourth. When analysing the expenditure on books and periodicals, it is found that in AUL, it has increased 10 fold from Rs. A lakhs to Rs. 4-0 lakhs during the study period, while in MKUL 12 times from Rs. 5.3 lakhs to Rs. 64 lakhs.

The average expenditure on books and periodicals under the annual plan shows a rising trend which is incresing from Rs. 1.4 lakhs to Rs. 13.4 lakhs in AUL and from Rs. 1.8 lakhs to 21 lakhs in MKUL. The annual average is found to be Rs. 6.3 lakhs and Rs. 9 lakhs in AUL and MKUL respectively. The above analysis clearly indicates that the expenditure on books and periodicals has been uniformly higher in MKUL than in AUL. This is attributed to the sanction of higher recurring grants to MKUL which is required for equipping and updating the newly established library with large number of books and periodicals.

The expenditure on staff salaries has shown an 8 times increase in AUL ranging from Rs. 1.4 lakhs to 11.38 lakhs during the period under study. As against this, in MKUL, it has ranged from Rs. 2 lakhs to Rs.15.6 lakhs recording an 8 fold increase. An analysis of the total expenditure on staff salaries indicates that MKUL has spent 41 per cent higher than that of AUL for staff salaries. This may be attributed to the fact that MKUL, being a new institution, requires more manpower to organise and administer the library services.

In absolute terms, the expenditure on miscellaneous items in AUL has increased from Rs. 0.3 lakhs to Rs.15 lakhs recording a 5 fold increase. As against this, it has increased from Rs.0.22 lakhs to 2.52 lakhs registering a 12 fold increase in MKUL. As in the case of the other two items of recurring expenditure, the amount spent on miscellaneous items by MKUL is also found to be higher than that of AUL by 46 per cent.

Reckoned in terms of the standards suggested by S.R. Ranganathan, it is found that the proportion of recurring expenditure on library materials has exceeded the suggested norm, while the proportion of expenditure on staff salaries has not reached the level suggested in both the libraries. But in view of the growing demands made for the various library services, a larger share of the recurring grants has to be channelised for the staff establishment.

Testing the Adequacy of the Financial Provision to AUL and MKUL

In order to measure the financial adequacy of the libraries, an analysis of the financial provision based on the enrollment of users is to be attempted. Here it is assumed that with the increase in the user population, there must be a corresponding increase in the financial provision for the libraries. The norms suggested by Guha and Jayaswal for computing the adequacy of library budget is given below:

Enrollment Within 500	*Per user cost (1978-79)*
Rs. 500 -3500	Rs. 100
Rs. 3501 - 10000	Rs. 350
Rs. 10001 - 35000	Rs. 300
Rs. 35001 - 50000	Rs. 250
Rs. 50001 - above	Rs. 200

The given norm is applicable for the whole sale price level of 1978-79, and it is use database to calculate the per user cost over the study period. The procedure is explained below:

* Dr. Ranganathan has suggested that the proportion of expenditure of University library budget on various items should be as under:

(a) Staff 50% (b) Books and other reading materials (c) Binding and other contingencies

Table 6
Cost Per User in AUL and MKUL

Plan Period	*AUL User Population*	*AUL Cost Per User Rs.*	*MKUL User population*	*MKUL Cost per user Rs.*	*Ratio of user population 2/4*
A	4994	44	205	1324	25:1
IV	6249	55	386	1440	16:1
V	7831	78	754	1107	10:1
VI	8173	165	1177	1464	7:1
VII	8645	202	1518	1768	6:1

Source : Computed.

Per user cost at the base year Whole sale price for Whole sale price for the base the current year.

An analysis of the adequacy of the financial provision of both AUL and MKUL based on the enrollment of users has been attempted. The cost per user or the per capita expenditure is used as a criteria to determine the adequacy of the allotment of fund's to the sample libraries. Relevant data are presented in Table 6.

A cursory glance at the table indicates that the cost per user of AUL has increased from Rs. 44 to Rs. 202 over the plan periods recording a 4.6 fold increase, while in MKUL it has increased from Rs. 1324 to Rs. 1768 marking a 1.3 fold increase. Comparatively, the per capita expenditure of MKUL is far higher than that of AUL while the proportion of variation ranges from 89 per cent to 97 per cent. This may be attributed to the receipt oflarge fund and relatively less number of enrollment of users.*

This position gets strengthened when the actual cost per user is compared with that of the norms suggested. The relevant data are given in Table 7.

It is striking to note that over the plan period the cost per user of AUL fails far short of the accepted norm, and the proportion of variation ranges from 73 per cent to 87 per cent upto the VI plan. As against this the cost per user in MKUL has exceeded the suggested norm, and the point of difference is

* The user enrollment of AUL has increased from 4994 to 8645 in AUL, while it has increased from 205 to 1518 in MKUL. The ratio of user population of the sample libraries is between 6:1 to 25:1 over the plan periods. In other words, for every 25 users in AUL there is only one user in MKUL during the Annual plan periods. This ratio has been decreasing over the successive plan periods. During the VII plan, for every 6 user in AUL, there is one in MKUL.

Source: Annual reports of the Annamalai University and Madurai Kamaraj University.

Table 7

Cost Per User as Per Norm (Rupees)

Plan Period	*AUL Cost per user as per norm*	*AUL Cost per user as per present position*	*AUL variation*	*MKUL Cost Per user as per norm*	*MKUL Cost per user as per present position*	*MKUL Variation*
A	1.66	44	-122	190	1324	+1134
IV	209	55	-154	283	1440	+1157
V	332	78	-254	264	1107	+843
VI	490	164	-326	490	1464	+974
VII	628	174	-454	628	1768	+1140

Sources : Computed.

between 65 per cent to 86 per cent during the period under review.

The above analysis throws light upon the inequity that exists in the provision of finance among the sample libraries. The reason for this inequity is not far to seek. Being a new university MKUL has added responsibility to build up the collections and service points from the base which involves large financial support. The relatively larger funds received by the MKUL confirms the hypothesis that new University Library has to be given greater financial provision so as to organise effective library collection and efficient service.

Notes

1. Nazir, Ahmad. *University Library Practices in developing countries.* London: KPI, 1984. p. 112.

2. A. Tejomurty. *Studies in Academic Librarianship*. Jaipur: Printwell, 1987. p. 77.

3. *Ibid.*, p. 92.

4. S.R. Ranganathan. "Academic Library System: Fourth planperiod". *Library Science*, Vol. 2, No. 4, December 1965. p. 227.

5. A.K. Guha and P.K. Jayaswal. "Budget Management in Libraries for higher education in Delhi - A comparative study". In: S.K. Kapoor (Ed) *Application of Management Techniques to Library and Information Systems*. Calcutta: IASLIC, 1979. p. 82.

6

Allocation of Finance Among the Various Units of the AUL and MKUL

A study of the trends in the finance of the sample libraries has indicated that there is inequity. This inequity is to be adjusted through the allocation process so as to maintain the quality of the sources and services. The allocation process involves the distribution of the funds among the major functional Units of the Library. They are (i) Acquisition Unit, (ii) Technical Unit and (iii) Service Unit. The function of the Acquisition unit is collection development in relation to the needs of the user. The Technical unit has to organise the acquired materials in order to make them readily available without any time lag. The function of the Service Unit is retrieving the required materials expeditiously. Though the functional characteristics of each unit is different, they are all directed towards the same target of meeting the information requirements of the users pinpointedly, expeditiously and exhaustively.

The allocation of finance to the Acquisition unit normally depends upon such factors as (i) student population, (ii) staff strength (iii) number of researchers, (iv) curricula, (v) new academic programmes, (vi) strength of existing collection and (vii) age of the university library. With the increase in the number of students, researchers and staff members, there must be a corresponding increase in the amount alloted to the Acquisition Unit. Guidelines for book-budget allocation to the different categories of users have been suggested by experts and expert committees. For instance, Dr. S.R. Ranganathan[1] has recommended Rs. 50 per student and Rs. 300 per teacher for the purpose of books and periodicals. The UGC's[2] Library Committee has suggested that a University Library with 5000 students and 500 teachers and research fellows should have a budget provision of Rs. 3.5 lakhs per annum, out of which Rs. 1.75 lakhs i.e. almost half would be spent on books, periodicals and kindred materials.* Regarding the curricula, the number of Departments of study, their sizes, courses offered, method of instruction and examination patterns are the important determinants in fund allocation.

High priority in the disbursement of funds has to be given to provide for an adequate collection, whenever new programmes are introduced. The strength of the existing collection should also be assessed. The weaker the collection is, the higher the priority rating is, which involves great apportionment. The Faculties/disciplines which have comparatively higher demand, require proportionately larger quota of funds.

While alloting funds to the Technical Unit, it is necessary to consider the quantum of work and the work force as the efficient running of this unit depends mostly on the availability

---

* That means the balance of 50 per cent of the budget provision alone should go to meet the expenditure on manpower requirements.

Table 1A

Allocation of Finance Among the Functional Units of AUL and MKUL (Rupees)

Plan Period	*Annamalai University Library*			*Madurai Kamaraj University Library*		
	Acquisition unit cost	*Technical unit cost*	*Service unit cost*	*Acquisition unit cost*	*Technical unit cost*	*Service unit cost*
A	484180 (73.5)	95490 (14.5)	78710 (12.0)	610490 (73.2)	110750 (13.4)	111820 (13.4)
IV	1345750 (78.0)	231530 (13.4)	147930 (8.6)	2229015 (79.5	329590 (11.7)	244410 (8.8)
V	2516480 (82.0)	345780 (11.2)	206840 (6.8)	3286635 (78.2)	554420 (13.2)	363600 (8.6)
VI	5901440 (86.5)	584205 (8.5)	333590 (5.0)	7421420 (83.9)	865430 (9.8)	556700 (6.3)
VII	4439660 (85.0)	508660 (9.7)	294800 (5.3)	6837790 (84.8)	733090 (9.1)	491620 (6.1)
Total	14687510 (83.9)	1765665 (10.0)	1061870 (6.1)	20385350 (82.3)	2593280 (10.5)	1768150 (7.2)

Source : Computed.

Table 1B
Annual Average Allocation of Finance among the Functional Units (Rupees)

	Annamalai University Library				*Madurai Kamaraj University Library*			
	Average acquisition unit cost	*Average technical unit cost*	*Average service unit cost*	*Average total cost*	*Average acquisition unit cost*	*Average technical unit cost*	*Average service unit cost*	*Average total cost*
A	161393 (100)	31830 (100)	26237 (100)	219460 (100)	203497 (too)	36917 (100)	37273 (100)	277687 (100)
IV	269150 (167)	46306 (145)	29856 (113)	345042 (157)	445803 (219)	65918 (179)	48882 (131)	560603 (202)
V	503296 (312)	69156 (217)	41368 (158)	613820 (280)	657327 (323)	110884 (300)	72720 (195)	840931 (303)
VI	1180288 (731)	116841 (367)	66718 (254)	1363848 (621)	1484284 (729)	173086 (469)	111340 (299)	1768710 (637)
VII	1479887 (917)	169553 (533)	98267 (375)	1741040 (793)	2279263 (1120)	244363 (662)	163873 (440)	2687467 (968)
Total	699405 (*33)	84079 (264)	*50565* (193)	834050 (380)	970730 (477)	123490 (335)	84198 (226)	1178413 (424)

(Figures in paranthesis represent Index Numbers)

Source: Computed.

of adequate number of staff members well versed in the process of documents, which implies sufficient allocation of funds on staff salaries. In the same way, for the successful functioning of the Service Unit, high calibre personnel, with proper training in readers[3] services is a necessity which again reiterates the need for larger allocation of finance for staff establishment.

In the light of the above theoretical background, an examination of the distribution of funds in the three units of the sample libraries is attempted. Data related to the allotment of funds among these three functional units are presented in Table 1.

Distribution of Funds among the Functional Units of the AUL and MKUL

It is striking to note that the allocation of funds to the Acquisition Unit has registered a 12.2 fold increase in both the library during the study period. It has increased from Rs. 4.84 lakhs to Rs. 59.01 lakhs in AUL and from Rs. 6.1 lakhs to Rs. 74.21 lakhs in MKUL over the years. Totally AUL has alloted Rs. 1.469 crores on the Acquisition Unit while MKUL has alloted Rs. 2.039 crores. The amount alloted to MKUL is higher than that of AUL and the amount of variation is Rs. 57 lakhs. This is explained by the fact that MKUL being a late comer has to spend larger amount on acquisition of materials.

The proportion of amount alloted to the Acquisition Unit has increased from 73.5 per cent to 85 per cent in AUL and from 73.2 per cent to 84.8 per cent in MKUL.

There appears to be no wide variation in the proportion of amount alloted to the Acquisition Unit in the sample libraries except during the V plan, when MKUL has registered a fall while AUL has registered a rise. This is attributed to the trend in the total allotment. During this period (V plan), AUL has registered 78 per cent increase as against 50 per cent increase in MKUL. Over the period, however, the proportion of finance alloted to the Acquisition unit is more or less the same in both the libraries. The amount alloted to the Technical unit of AUL has registered a 5 fold increase from Rs. 0.9 lakhs to Rs. 5 lakhs as against a 7 fold increase from Rs. 1.1 lakhs to Rs. 7.3 lakhs by the MKUL. The annual average expenditure of the Technical unit also has increased from Rs. 0.3 lakhs to Rs. 1.7 lakhs in AUL and from Rs. 0.4 lakhs to Rs. 2.4 lakhs in MKUL. In terms of proportions, there is a falling trend in both the Libraries which may be due to the allotment made for the library materials necessitated by the rise in the number of departments and enrollment of students.* The allocation of finance to the Service Unit of the AUL has increased from Rs. 0.8 lakhs to Rs. 2.9 lakh registering a 5 fold increase while that of MKUL from Rs. 1.1 lakhs to Rs. 5 lakhs. The annual plan average of the Service Unit of both the libraries has also exhibited a rising trend from Rs. 0.37 lakhs to Rs. 16.4 lakhs in MKUL. But the proportion of the amount alloted to the Service Unit of both the libraries has recorded a declining trend.

From the above it is clear that among the three Units of the Library, the Acquisition Unit has been given greater proportion of funds in both the Libraries.

Now, it is interesting to find out the extent to which the allocation of funds among the various units of the library has satisfied the standard criteria. According to Dix, two-thirds of the annual expenditure of the University Library should go to cover the cost of acquisitions and the remaining third for the

---

* The number of Departments in the AUL has increased from 25 in the Annual plans to 45 in the VII plan, as against 9 in the Annual plans to 20 in the VII plan in MKUL. There is also a sharp rise in the enrollment of students in AUL which has increased from 4746 to 9033 while that of MKUL from 170 to 1738.

Source: Annual Reports of the Annamalai University and Madurai Kamaraj University.

other services that will make the collection perform its appropriate functions.

A close analysis of Table 1 reveals that AUL and MKUL have satisfied well the standard criteria suggested by Dix. It is heartening to note that both the libraries have exceeded the norm by allocating more than 20 per cent of their budget to the Acquisition Unit. It is appreciable that the Service Units have been managed within the proportion of amount sanctioned to these Units.

To assess the allocation efficiency of each functional Unit, an indepth study is essential. An attempt has therefore been made to analyse the (i) allotment of funds among the cost components of the three individual units of the sample Libraries and their level of performance.

Notes

1. S.R. Ranganathan. "Academic Library System". *Library Science with Slant to Documentation*. Vol. 2, 1965. p. 319.

2. UGC, India. *University and College Libraries*. New Delhi: UGC, 1965, pp. 72-73.

3. Nazir Ahmad. *University Library Practices in Developing Countries*. London: KPI, 1984. pp. 103-104.

7

Evaluation of the Acquisition Unit of the AUL and MKUL

Evaluation of the Acquisition Unit centres around two main aspects viz: (i) Allocation adequacy and (ii) collection development. Allocation adequacy is determined in terms of the proportion of amount allocated to the cost components of the Acquisition Unit, which are broadly classified into (i) material cost, (ii) labour cost and (iii) miscellaneous cost. The material cost includes cost of acquiring monographs, serials and other reading materials. Labour cost consists of the cost of payment to the professional and non-professional staff (who selects, verifies request, orders monographs and serial titles, types and files orders, receives and pays for titles ordered, and finally records expenditure and sends titles on to the catalogue Department). Miscellaneous cost indicates the cost of payment to the building furniture and equipment associated with the Acquisition Unit.

Among the three cost items, material cost has to be alloted a high percentage of the fund, as it would be essential to keep pace with the unprecedented influx of printed literature and to

Table 1
Cost Components of the Acquisition Unit (Rupees)

Plan period	Annamalai University Library			Madurai Kamaraj University Library		
	Material cost	Labour cost	Miscellaneous cost	Material cost	Labour Cost	Miscellaneous cost
A	411040 (85)	55200 (11)	17940 (4.0)	525200 (86.0)	65800 (11.0)	188900 (3.0)
IV	1189900 (88)	125600 (9.5)	302500 (2.5)	200700 (89.9)	188300 (8.4)	36015 (1.7)
V	2264600 (90)	219200 (9.0)	32680 (1.0)	2956920 (90.0)	288200 (8.8)	41515 (1.2)
VI	5439275 (92)	425700 (7)	36465 (1.0)	6926200 (93.3)	451000 (6.0)	44220 (0.7)
VI I	4040800 (91)	374420 (8.4)	24449 (0.6)	6425600 (94.0)	385500 (5.6)	26590 (0.4)
Total	13345615 (90.0)	1200120 (8.1)	141775 (i.0)	18839200 (92.4)	1378800 (6.8)	167230 (O.S)

(Figures in paranthesis represent proportions)

Source: Computed.

build a comprehensive collection of materials. Secondly, a reasonable proportion has to be alloted for the requisite staff salaries so as to carry out the job promptly and efficiently. The balance can be alloted to the miscellaneous items.

The cost components of the Acquisition Unit of AUL and MKUL are illustrated in Table 1. It is noteworthy that the material cost of AUL has recorded a 9.8 fold increase from Rs. 1.37 lakhs in the Annual plan to Rs. 13.47 lakhs in the VII plan. As against this, MKUL has registered a 12.2 fold increase from Rs. 1.75 lakhs in the Annual plan period to Rs. 21 lakhs in the VII plan periods. The proportion of material expenditure in MKUL is larger than that of AUL which may be explained by the fact that being a new University library, it has to build up the collection from the base.

The increase in the proportion of expenditure on staff establishment in AUL is due to the larger number of staff maintained to cope with the increased volumes of work. However, the expenditure on staff establishment in absolute terms is relatively lesser in AUL. This is explained by the staff pattern in AUL, where most of the staff are temporary.

The cost of miscellaneous items is only a non-recurring expenditure such as expenditure on building, furniture and equipment, and hence the depreciation value is taken into account. The expenditure on miscellaneous items in AUL has increased from Rs. 0.19 lakhs to Rs. 2.4 lakhs, and in MKUL from Rs. 0.19 lakhs to Rs. 2.7 lakhs. A look into the absolute terms indicate that the cost on miscellaneous items of MKUL has been higher than that of AUL throughout the plan period. The variation ranges from 0.05 points to 21 points in the Annual, IV and VI Five year plan periods and 27 points in the V plan period. This can be explained by the fact that MKUL, being established during the late sixtees has to spend largely on the procurement of building, furniture and equipment. This has necessitated MKUL to set apart greater depreciation than that

Table 2A
Distribution of Material Expenditure by Formats in AUL and MKUL (Rupees)

Plan	*Book Expenditure*		*Periodical Expenditure*		*Total Expenditure*	
period	*AUL*	*MKUL*	*AUL*	*MKUL*	*AUL*	*MKUL*
A	291900	112600	116140	113200	111010	525800
IV	839900	1512100	350000	162300	1189900	2001700
V	1311600	2096600	950000	860320	2261600	2956920
VI	3773775	3921100	1665500	3005100	5139275	6926200
VII	2355300	3361950	1685500	3060650	1010800	6125600
Total	8578175	11337650	1767110	7501570	13315615	18839220

Source: Computed.

of AUL which is having relatively old equipments and hence, a lower absolute amount on miscellaneous items.

Distribution of Material Expenditure by Formats in AUL and MKUL

Books and periodicals constitute the major items of library materials. Hence, an analysis of the distribution of funds among these items merits attention. The data relating to the book and periodical expenditure is presented in Table 2A. It is revealing to note that book expenditure of AUL and MKUL has recorded an 8 fold increase over the years. The book expenditure of AUL has increased from Rs. 2.94 lakhs in the Annual plan period to Rs. 37.73 lakhs in the VI plan period: while that of MKUL has increased from Rs. 4.12 lakhs to Rs. 39.2 lakhs. Though the rate of increase in the book expenditure is the same in both AUL and MKUL, the actual amount exhibits a marked difference. This may be understood by the fact that while AUL has alloted a total of Rs. 85.78 lakhs on books, MKUL has alloted 1.5 times higher at Rs. 113.37 lakhs.

Expenditure on periodicals has also registered sizeable increases over the years. Total expenditure on periodicals of AUL has recorded sharp increases especially during the last 3 plan periods. The rate of growth of expenditure on periodicals has shot up by 14.5 times in AUL and 22 times in MKUL. The range of difference in the expenditure on periodicals by the MKUL varies from 32 points to 82 points. Totally expenditure on periodicals during the plan period works out to be Rs. 47.67 lakhs in AUL while it is higher at Rs. 75 lakhs in MKUL.*

The total material expenditure of the AUL has increased from Rs. 4.1 lakhs to Rs. 40.4 lakhs during the study period recording a 10 fold increase, while that of MKUL has increased from Rs. 5.26 lakhs to Rs. 64.26 lakhs registering more than a

---

* This difference is due to the UGC which has provided more funds to the MKUL for the purchase of back volumes.

Table 2B
Average Expenditure on Books and Periodicals (Rupees)

Plan Period	Average Book Expenditure		Average Periodical Expenditure		Average Total Material Expenditure	
	AUL	MKUL	AUL	MKUL	AUL	MKUL
A	98300 (100)	137537 (100)	38713 (100)	37733 (100)	137013 (100)	175667 (100)
IV	167980 (170)	308480 (224)	70000 (181)	92460 (245)	237980 (174)	400940 (229)
V	262920 (267)	419320 (305)	190000 (491)	172064 (456)	452920 (330)	591384 (337)
VI	754755 (768)	784220 (570)	333100 (860)	601020 (1593)	1087855 (794)	1385240 (790)
VII	785100 (799)	1121650 (816)	561833 (1451)	1020217 (2704)	1346933 (983)	2141867 (1222)
Total	408500 (416)	539888 (393)	227007 (586)	357218 (942)	635505 (464)	897106 (512)

(Figures in paranthesis represent proportions)

Source: Computed.

Table 2C

Proportion of Books and Periodical Expenditure

Plan Period	*Book Expenditure*		*Periodical Expenditure*	
	AUL	*MKUL*	*AUL*	*MKUL*
A	72.0	78.5	28.0	21.5
IV	70.5	77.0	29.5	23.0
V	58.0	71.0	42.0	29.0
VI	69.4	56.6	30.6	43.4
VII	58.2	52.4	41.8	47.6
Total	64.3	60.2	35.7	39.8

Source: Computed.

12 fold increase. Over the whole period, the total material expenditure of MKUL has been higher at Rs. 1.88 crores than that of AUL (Rs. 1.33 crores). The difference being Rs. 55 lakhs. This is understandable that MKUL being a late comer, has to develop a full-fledged collection of the past and current publications.

Average Expenditure on Books and Periodicals (Table 2B)

The average expenditure on books by AUL and MKUL has recorded an 8 fold increase. It has increased from Rs. 0.98 lakhs in the Annual plan period to Rs. 7.8 lakhs in the VII plan in AUL and from Rs.1.37 lakhs to 11.2 lakhs in MKUL. Taking the whole period under review, the average expenditure on books by the MKUL is (Rs. 5.39 lakhs) higher than that of AUL (Rs. 4 lakhs).

The average expenditure on periodicals by the AUL has recorded 14.5 fold increase from Rs. 0.38 lakhs in the Annual plan to Rs. 5.6 lakhs in the VII plan while that of MKUL has registered 27 fold increase from Rs. 0.37 lakhs to Rs. 10.2 lakhs. Totally, the average expenditure on periodicals for the period under review works out to Rs. 2.27 lakhs for AUL and Rs. 3.57 lakhs for MKUL.

It is clear that the average expenditure on books and periodicals in the VI and VII plan has far exceeded the total average in both the University Libraries.

Proportion of Book and Periodical Expenditure (Vide Table 2C)

The proportion of books and periodicals expenditure reveals that expenditure on books by both the University Libraries under successive plan has recorded relatively lesser proportions, while the proportion of expenditure on periodicals has registered significant increase. This is explained by the (i) increase in the number of journal publications and their increasing costs and (ii) the added emphasis given to research.

Distribution of Material Expenditure by Discipline

An analysis of the distribution of total material expenditure by discipline will reflect the emphasis given to the various Faculties by the two University Libraries. Details of material expenditure by Disciplines such as (i) Arts, (ii) Science and Technology, (iii) Oriental Languages and Linguistics and (iv) Education is given in Table 3A.

It is revealing to note that the material expenditure on Arts in AUL was at Rs. 0.9 lakhs while that of MKUL was 3 times higher at Rs. 2.67 lakhs. The expenditure on Arts in AUL has more than doubled in the last three plan periods while that of MKUL only in the IV and VI plan periods. Throughout the period under review, the expenditure on Arts by the MKUL has been relatively higher than that of AUL, and the proportion of variation ranges from 196 percent to 387 percent. As a result, the total material expenditure on Arts by MKUL is nearly four times higher at Rs. 94.53 lakhs than that of Rs. 25.61 lakhs in AUL over the plan period. This is due to the increase in the number of Departments in the Faculty of Arts and the corresponding rise in the number of students, researchers and staff members in MKUL.

Expenditure on the Faculty of Science and Technology, on the other hand reveals the opposite trend (vide Table 3A). It may be observed that the material expenditure on S & T in MKUL was Rs. 1.96 lakhs during the Annual plan periods, while that of AUL was 1.5 times higher at Rs. 2.78 lakhs. In AUL, the material expenditure on S & T has more than, doubled in all the successive plan periods but it is found to be doubled in MKUL only in the IV and VI plan periods. AUL has spent relatively larger amount on S & T than that of MKUL and the proportion of variation has ranged from 10 points to 40 points. As a result,' the total material expenditure on S & T over the plan periods by the AUL is 1.2 times higher at Rs. 1 crore than that of

Table 3A
Distribution of Material Expenditure by Discipline (Rupees)

Plan period	*Faculty of Arts*		*Faculty of S & T*		*Faculty of OL & Linguistics*		*Faculty of Education*	
	AUL	*MKUL*	*AUL*	*MKUL*	*AUL*	*MKUL*	*AUL*	*MKUL*
A	90400	267900	272,000	196630	30940	52770	11700	8500
IV	203800	992975	879000	822670	79000	149900	28000	39155
V	354600	1451540	1660000	1242100	195000	213990	55000	49290
VI	1058775	3593700	^155000	2988455	159500	282645	66000	61400
VII	854000	3146950	3058300	3034760	86000	202200	42500	41700
Total	2561578	9453065	10030300	8284605	550^0	901505	203200	200045

Source: Computed.

Table 3B

Proportion of Material Expenditure by Discipline

Plan Period	*Faculty of Arts*		*Faculty of S & T*		*Faculty of OL & Linguistics*		*Faculty of Education*	
	AUL	*MKUL*	*AUL*	*MKUL*	*AUL*	*MKUL*	*AUL*	*MKUL*
A	22.0	67.6	7.5	2.9	51.1	37.4	10.0	1.6
IV	17.1	73.9	6.6	2.4	49.5	41.0	7.5	2.0
V	15.7	73.3	8.6	2.4	49.0	42.0	7.3	1.7
VI	19.5	76.4	2.9	1.2	51.9	43.1	4.0	1.0
VII	21.1	75.7	2.1	1.1	49.0	47.0	3.1	0.7
Total	19.2	75.2	4.1	1.5	50.2	44.0	4.8	1.0

Source: Computed.

Rs. 52.84 lakhs in MKUL. This is attributed to the expansion of Departments in the Faculty of S & T in AU.*

In the case of Oriental Languages and Linguistics AUL has spent Rs. 5.5 lakhs over the plan periods on procurement of materials while MKUL has spent Rs. 9.1 lakhs. As regards total expenditure on Education, it is almost the same at Rs. 2 lakhs in both the libraries. The lesser allotment made on the Faculty of OL and Linguistics and Education by both the Libraries may be attributed to the limited number of enrollments in these Faculties.

The proportion of material expenditure by discipline (vide Table 3B) exhibit, clearly the degree of importance attached to the different faculties by the sample libraries. It is interesting to note that AUL has shared one-fifth on Arts and two-thirds to three-fourths on Science and Technology over the plan periods. The other small share (5.5 per cent) has been spent on the Faculty of Oriental Languages and Linguistics and Education.

In the same way, MKUL has spent 50 percent on Arts, 37 percent to 47.2 percent on S & T and 10 to 3.1 percent on OL & Linguistics during the period under review. Thus the above analysis has thrown light on the fact that both the Libraries have given priority to the Faculty of S & T, followed by Arts and other Faculties in allocating the book-fund (vide Table 3D). It is also revealing to note that the sample libraries have observed the general trend in the allocation of funds among the Faculties.**

---

* In AUL the number of departments in the Faculty of S &T has increased from Eleven to Twenty seven during the periodunder review. While in MKUL it has increased from three to seven.

** In recent times, a very substantial and increasing portion of the acquisition budget has been spent on materials in Science and Technology due to the heightened intensity of academic research in S & T.

Source:Annual Reports of the Annamalai University and Madurai Kamaraj University.

Table 3C

Growth Rate of Material Expenditure by Discipline

Plan period	Faculty of Arts		Faculty of S & T		Faculty Ling of OL & uistics		Faculty of Education	
	AUL	*MKUL*	*AUL*	*MKUL*	*AUL*	*MKUL*	*AUL*	*MKUL*
A	100	100	100	100	100	100	100	100
IV	135	222	190	251	153	170	144	276
V	235	325	358	379	378	243	282	348
VI	703	S05	897	912	309	321	338	433
VII	945	1175	1100	1543	278	383	363	491
Total	405	504	515	602	254	244	248	336

(Figures in paranthesis represent proportions)

Source: Computed.

Table 3D
Comparison of Material Expenditure by Discipline in AUL and MKUL (Rupees)

Plan Period	Faculty of Arts		Faculty of S & T		Faculty of OL Linguistics		Faculty of Education	
	AUL	MKUL	AUL	MKUL	AUL	MKUL	AUL	MKUL
A	90400 (22.0)	267900 (51.0)	27S000 (67.6)	196630 (37.4)	30940 (7.5)	52770 (10.0)	11700 (2.9)	8500 (1.6)
IV	203800 (17.1)	992975 (49.5)	879000 (73.9)	822670 (41.0)	79000 (6.6)	149900 (7.5)	28000 (2.4)	39155 (2.0)
V	354600 (15.7)	145154 0 (49.0)	1660000 (73.3)	1242100 (42.0)	195000 (8.6)	213990 (7.3)	55000 (2.4)	49290 (1.7)
VI	1058775 (19.5)	359370 0 (51.9)	^155000 (76.4)	2988455 (43.1)	159500 (2.9)	282645 (4.0)	66000 (1.2)	61400 (1.0)
VII	854000 (21.1)	314695 0 (49.0)	3058300 (75.7)	3034750 (47.2)	86000 (2.1)	202200 (3.1)	42500 (1.1)	41700 (0.7)
Total	2561575 (19.2)	945306 5 (50.2)	10030300 (75.2)	8284605 (44.0)	550440 (4.1)	901505 (4.8)	203200 (1.5)	200045 (1.0)

(Figures in paranthesis represent proportions)

Source: Computed.

The growth rate of expenditure in AUL is almost uniform in all the plan periods (vide Table 3C). As already seen, the growth rate of material expenditure of MKUL over the AUL is higher particularly in S & T and Arts. When comparing the growth rate of material expenditure of the sample Libraries with that of the standards,"* it is found that both AUL and MKUL have not satisfied the norms suggested.

Distribution of Book Expenditure by Discipline

An analysis of the book expenditure will throw light on the relative importance attached to the acquisition of monographs among the different faculties. The relevant data is given in Table 4A. It is revealing to note that the book expenditure on Arts by AUL has recorded nearly 12 fold increse over the years from Rs. 0.71 lakhs in the Annual plan period to Rs. 5.38 lakhs in the VI plan period, while that of MKUL has registered a 10 fold increase from Rs. 2 lakhs to Rs. 20.5 lakhs. But the total of MKUL is nearly three times higher at Rs. 57.56 lakhs than that of AUL which is only Rs. 19.5 lakhs.

In the case of the Faculty of S & T, book expenditure of AUL has registered 15 fold increase while MKUL has recorded only 10 fold increase over the plan periods. It has increased from Rs.1.86 lakhs in the Annual plan period to Rs. 27.7 lakhs in the VI plan period in AUL and from Rs. 1.59 lakhs to Rs. 16.57 lakhs in MKUL. Totally AUL has spent Rs. 61.15 lakhs on the Faculty of S & T for the procurement of books while MKUL has spent Rs. 8.71 lakhs. Thus the book expenditure on S & T by the AUL is higher than that of MKUL. This is explained by the introduction of new courses in Engineering, Agriculture and Medicine during this period.

Expenditure on books of OL & Linguistics in AUL and MKUL has exhibited a 4 fold increase over the years. It has

---

* To assess the growth rate of Book Budget, Ehikhamenor has advocated 10 to 15 percent annual increase inorder to cope with the rapidly growing volume and cost of publications.

Table 4A
Distribution of Book Expenditure by Discipline (Rupees)

Plan Period	Faculty of Arts		Faculty of 5 & T		Faculty of OL & Linguistics		Faculty of Education		Total Book Expenditure	
	AUL	MKUL	AUL	MKUL	AUL	MKUL	AUL	MKUL	AUL	MKUL
A	71900 (24.4)	206200 (50.0)	186000 (63.0)	159550 (38.7)	27000 (9.2)	40150 (9.7)	10000 (3.4)	6700 (1.6)	294900 (100)	412600 (100)
IV	153900 (18.3)	751775 (48.7)	601000 (71.5)	656230 (42.5)	60000 (7.1)	103980 (6.7)	25000 (3.1)	30415 (2.1)	839900 (100)	1542400 (100)
V	254600 (19.4)	1003140 (47.8)	^0000 (67.0)	927770 (44.3)	140000 (10.6)	128940 (6.1)	^0000 (3.0)	36750 (1.8)	1314600 (100)	2096600 (100)
VI	838775 (22.2)	2050900 (52.3)	2770000 (73.4)	1656935 (42.3)	120000 (3.2)	169515 (4.3)	^5000 (1.2)	43750 (1.1)	3773775 (100)	3921100 (100)
VII	631980 (26.4)	1744575 (51.8)	1678025 (70.1)	1470975 (43.7)	54780 (2.3)	121200 (3.6)	30360 (1.2)	28200 (0.9)	2392100 (100)	3364950 (100)
Total	1951155 (22.6)	5756590 (50.8)	6115025 (71.0)	4871460 (43.0)	401780 (4.7)	5637^5 (5.0)	150360 (1.7)	145815 (1.2)	8615275 (100)	11337650 (100)

(Figures in Paranthesis Represent Proportions)

Source: Computed.

increased from Rs. 0.27 lakhs in the Annual plan period to Rs. 1.2 lakhs in the VI plan periods in AUL and from Rs. 0.4 lakhs to Rs. 1.69 lakhs in MKUL. Totally, MKUL has expended Rs. 5.63 lakhs in purchase of books for OL and Linguistics while AUL has spent Rs. 4 lakhs. Thus, book expenditure on OL & Linguistics by MKUL is higher than that of AUL and the proportion of variation ranges from 40 points to 70 points.

In the same way, the book expenditure on Education in AUL has recorded nearly a 5 fold increase while MKUL has registered a 7 fold increase over the plan periods. It has increased from Rs. 0.1 lakhs to Rs. 0.45 lakhs in AUL and from Rs. 0.60 lakhs to Rs. 9.43 lakhs in MKUL. The total book expenditure on Education has worked out to be Rs. 1.5 lakhs in AUL and Rs.1.45 lakhs in MKUL. In this regard, there is not much difference between the two Libraries.

Average Book Expenditure by Discipline (vide Table 4B)

In the Faculty of Arts, the average expenditure of AUL has doubled from Rs. 0.23 lakhs to Rs. 0.5 lakhs in the V plan and reached the peak of Rs. 2.1 lakhs in the VII plan while that of MKUL has recorded an 8 fold increase over the plan periods from Rs. 0.68 lakhs in the Annual plan to Rs. 5.8 lakhs in the VII plan. Similarly in the Faculty of S & T, AUL has expended an average of Rs. 0.62 lakhs to Rs. 5.59 lakhs over the plan periods, thus recording an 8 fold increase while that of MKUL has spent an average of Rs. 0.5 lakhs to Rs. 4.9 lakhs registering a 9 fold increase. But a reverse trend is observed in the average expenditure on OL & Linguistics by the AUL. It has marked a 3 fold increase from Rs. 0.09 lakhs to 0.28 lakhs upto the V plan period, after which it has declined due to the stoppage of Special Grants from the UGC.

Taking the whole period under review, the annual average expenditure of MKUL is Rs. 5.39 lakhs which is higher than that of AUL at Rs. 4.9 lakhs, the difference has varied from *OA*

Table 4B
Average Book Expenditure by Discipline in AUL and MKUL(Rupees)

	Faculty of Arts		*Faculty of S & T*		*Faculty of OL & Linguistics*		*Faculty of Education*		*Total*	
Plan Period	*AUL*	*MKUL*	*AUL*	*MKUL*	*AUL*	*MKUL*	*AUL*	*MKUL*	*AUL*	*MKUL*
A	23967	68733	62000	53183	900	13383	3333	2233	98300	137533
	(100)	(100)	(100)	(100)	(100)	(100)	(100)	(100)	(100)	(100)
IV	30780	150355	120200	131246	12000	20796	5000	6083	167980	308480
	(128)	(219)	(194)	(247)	(133)	(155)	(150)	(272)	(171)	(224)
V	50920	200628	176000	185554	28000	25788	8000	7350	262920	419320
	(212)	(292)	(284)	(349)	(311)	(193)	(240)	(329)	(267)	(320)
VI	167755	410180	554000	331387	24000	33903	9000	8750	754755	784220
	(700)	(597)	(894)	(623)	(267)	(253)	(270)	(392)	(768)	(570)
VII	210660	581525	559342	490325	18260	40400	10120	9400	797367	1121650
	(879)	(846)	(802)	(922)	(203)	(302)	(304)	(421)	(811)	(816)
Total	92912	274123	291192	231974	19132	26847	7160	6944	410251	539888
	(388)	(399)	(470)	(436)	(213)	(201)	(215)	(311)	(417)	(393)

(Figures in paranthesis represent proportions)

Source: Computed.

Table 4C
Proportion of Book Expenditure by Discipline (Percentage)

Plan periods	Annamalai University Library				Madurai Kamaraj University Library			
	Faculty of Arts	Faculty of S & T	Faculty of OL & Linguistcs	Faculty of Education	Faculty of Arts	Faculty of S & T	Faculty of OL & Linguistics	Faculty of Education
A	24.4	63.0	9.2	3.4	*50.0*	35.5	9.7	1.6
IV	18.3	71.5	7.1	3.1	48.7	42.5	6.7	2.1
V	19.4	67.0	10.6	3.0	47.8	44.3	6.1	1.8
VI	22.2	73.4	3.2	1.2	52.3	42.3	4.3	1.1
VII	26.64	70.1	2.3	1.2	51.8	43.7	3.6	0.9
Total	22.7	71.0	4.7	1.7	50.8	43.0	5.0	1.2

Source: Computed.

points to 59 points. It is also clear that the average book expenditure on the Arts and Science Faculties has registered mainfold increase in the last two plan periods in both the Libraries.

The proportion of book expenditure on Arts in the sample libraries has also shown increases during the VI and VII plan periods due to the introduction of new job oriented courses such as Library Science, Management Science, etc. Throughout the plan periods, AUL has committed more than 70 percent of its total book expenditure on S & T, while the share is 43 percent in MKUL. This is explained by the number of Departments in the Faculty of S & T in both the Universities. Due to a fall in the enroll merit, the proportion of book expenditure on OL & Linguistics declined from the V plan period in AUL and MKUL. The same trend is discernible in the Faculty of Education also.

Distribution of Periodicals Expenditure by Discipline (vide Table 5)

An analysis of periodical expenditure will explain the priority given to research activity in each Faculty. The periodical expenditure on Arts has recorded a 12 fold increase from Rs. 0.18 lakhs in the Annual Plan to Rs. 2.2 lakhs in the VII plan in AUL, while MKUL has registered 25 fold increase from Rs. 0.61 lakhs, to Rs. 13.8 lakhs. Totally, AUL has spent Rs. 47 lakhs on periodicals while MKUL has spent Rs. 75 lakhs. The increase in the periodical expenditure by the MKUL is attributed to the growth in the number of research departments and in take of scholars in the Arts Faculty of MKUL. But in the case of expenditure on periodicals in S&T AUL has recorded 15 fold increase from Rs. 0.92 lakhs in the Annual Plan period to Rs. 13.8 lakhs in the VII plan, while that of MKUL has registered a 42 fold, increase from Rs. 0.37 lakhs to Rs. 15.63 lakhs. The total periodical expenditure of S & T works out to be Rs. 39.15 lakhs in AUL and Rs. 34.13 lakhs in MKUL. Though the rate of increase is higher in MKUL, the total amount spent on the

Table 5

Distribution of Periodicals Expenditure by Discipline

Plan period	*Faculty of Arts*		*Faculty of S & T*		*Faculty of OL& Linguistics*		*Faculty of Education*		*Total periodical expenditure*	
	AUL	*MKUL*	*AUL*	*MKUL*	*AUL*	*MKUL*	*AUL*	*MKUL*	*AUL*	*MKUL*
A	18500	61700	92080	37080	3940	12620	1700	1800	116140	113200
	(15.9)	(54.5)	(79.2)	(32.8)	(3.4)	(11.1)	(1.5)	(1.6)	(100)	(100)
IV	50000	241200	278000	166440	19000	45920	3000	8740	350000	462300
	(14.3)	(52.2)	(78.4)	(36.0)	(5.4)	(9.9)	(0.9)	(1.9)	(100)	(100)
V	100000	448400	780000	314330	55000	85050	5000	12540	950000	850320
	(10.5)	(52.1)	(82.1)	(36.5)	(5.8)	(9.9)	(1.6)	(1.5)	(100)	(100)
VI	220000	1542800	1385000	1331520	39500	113130	21000	17650	1665500	3005100
	(13.2)	(51.3)	(83.2)	(44.3)	(2.4)	(3.8)	(1.2)	(0.6)	(100)	(100)
VII	222020	1402375	1380275	1563375	31220	81000	12140	13500	1645665	3060650
	(13.5)	(45.8)	(83.9)	(51.1)	(1.9)	(2.6)	(0J)	(0.5)	(100)	(100)
Total	610520	3696475	3915275	3413145	148660	337720	52840	54230	4727295	7501570
	(12.9)	(49.3)	(82.8)	(45.5)	(3.1)	(4.5)	(1.2)	(0.7)	(100)	(100)

(Figures in paranthesis represent proportions)

Source: Computed.

Table 6

Distribution of Materials Expenditure by Format and Discipline by Annamalai University Library (Percentage)

Plan period	*Faculty of Arts*			*Faculty of S & T*			*Faculty of OL & Linguistics*			*Faculty of Education*			*Total*		
	Books	*Periodicals*	*Total*	*Books*	*Periodicals*	*Total*	*Books*	*Periodicals*	*Total*	*Books*	*Periodicals*	*Total*	*Books*	*Periodicals*	*Total*
A	17.5	4.5	22.0	45.2	22.4	67.6	6.6	1.0	7.5	2.4	0.4	2.9	71.7	28.3	100
IV	12.9	4.2	17.1	51.5	23.4	73.9	5.0	1.6	6.6	2.1	0.3	2.4	70.6	29.4	100
V	11.2	4.4	15.7	38.9	34.4	73.3	6.2	2.4	8.6	1.8	0.7	2.4	58.0	42.0	100
VI	15.4	4.0	19.5	51.0	25.5	76.4	2.2	0.7	2.9	0.5	0.4	1.2	69.4	30.6	100
VII	15.6	5.5	21.1	41.5	34.2	75.7	1.4	0.8	2.1	0.7	0.3	1.1	59.2	40.8	100
Total	14.5	4.5	19.1	45.8	29.2	75.0	3.1	1.1	4.2	1.5	0.4	1.9	64.6	36.4	100

Source: Computed.

Table 7
Distribution of Materials Expenditure by Format and Discipline Categories, Madurai Kamaraj University Library

Plan period	*Faculty of Arts*			*Faculty of S &*			*Faculty of OL & Linguistics*			*Faculty of Education*			*Total*		
	Books	*Periodicals*	*Total*	*Books*	*Periodicals*	*Total*	*Books*	*Periodicals*	*Total*	*Books*	*Periodicals*	*Total*	*Books*	*Periodicals*	*Total*
A	39.2	11.7	51.0	30.3	7.1	37.4	7.7	2.4 1	0.0	1.3	0.3	1.6	78.5	21.5	100
IV	37.5	12.1	49.5	32.7	8.3	41.0	5.2	2.3	7.5	1.5	0.4	2.0	77.0	23.0	100
V	33.9	15.2	49.0	31.4	10.6	42.0	4.4	2.9	7.3	1.2	0.4	1.7	70.9	29.1	100
VI	29.6	22.3	51.9	24.0	19.2	43.1	2.4	1.6	4.0	0.6	0.3	1.0	56.6	43.4	100
VII	27.2	21.8	49.0	22.9	24.3	47.2	1.9	1.3	3.1	0.4	0.2	0.7	52.4	47.6	100
Total	30.5	19.6	50.1	25.9	18.1	44.0	3.0	1.8	4.8	O.S	0.3	1.1	60.2	38.8	100

Source: Computed.

periodicals of S & T by the AUL is higher than that of MKUL. The difference ranges from 0.4 points to 148 points.

In the case of OL and Linguistics, the periodical expenditure has registered sharp increases in both the libraries till the V plan periods. This may be due to the receipt of special grants by the Department of Linguistics in AUL consequent on the upgradation of this Department as a Centre of Advanced Study and Research. As against these, periodical expenditure of the Faculty of Education is almost identical in both the libraries.

Thus, it is clear from the above analysis that AUL has spent 82.9 percent of its periodical expenditure on S & T, 12.9 percent on Arts, 3.1 percent on Oriental Languages and Linguistics and 1.2 percent on Education. As against this, MKUL has distributed 49.3 percent for Arts, 45.5 percent for S & T, 4.5 percent for Oriental Languages and Linguistics and 0.7 percent for Education. In both the Libraries, a major share is alloted to Arts, S & T (35%) in order to cope with the expanding research programmes in these fields.

Distribution of Material Expenditure by Format and Discipline Categories in AUL and MKUL

An analysis of the expenditure pattern across format will indicate the importance attached to each one of the format among the various faculties. The data relevant to the book and periodical expenditure among the faculties in both the university libraries are presented in Table 6 & 7. A glance at the Table will reveal that a lion's share of the material expenditure has been alloted for the purchase of books rather than periodicals. It is interesting to note that AUL has committed 64.6 percent for books and 35.4 percent for periodicals while MKUL has expended 60.2 percent for books and 39.8 percent for periodicals.

Of this, the book expenditure on Science and Technology in AUL account for 70.9 percent, Arts 22.45 percent, Oriental Languages and Linguistics 4.8 percent and Education

1.85 percent over the plan periods. As against this, MKUL has allocated its book expenditure in the order of 50.7 percent for Arts, 43 percent for S & T, 5 percent for Oriental Languages and Linguistics and 1.3 percent for Education. The concentration of material funds on books in both the libraries reflects the fact that the Academic Libraries have to support, apart from research, the instructional programmes of the Universities at the graduate and postgraduate levels.

Both the libraries have shared nearly two-fifths of their material funds for subscribing to periodicals during the study periods. Of these, AUL has allocated a larger portion for subscribing to the periodicals on S & T (2.3%) followed by Arts (12.7%), Oriental Languages and Linguistics (3.1%) and Education (1.2%). As against this, MKUL has spent almost equal proportion on Arts (49.2%) and S & T (45.5%) followed by Oriental Languages and Linguistics (4.5%) and Education (2.8%).

It is apparent from the above analysis that AUL has committed 64.6 percent for books and 35.4 percent for periodicals. From this the Faculty of Arts has received 14.5 percent for books and 4.5 percent for periodicals; the Faculty of S & T has received 45.8 percent for books and 29.2 percent for periodicals; the Faculty of Oriental Languages and Linguistics has received 3.1 percent and 1.1 percent respectively for books and periodicals; and the Faculty of Education has received 1.5 percent for books and 0.4 percent for periodicals.

Similarly, the MKUL has expended 59.2 percent for books and 39.8 percent for periodicals. Of these, the Faculty of Arts has received 30.5 percent for books and 19.6 percent for periodicals; the Faculty of S & T has received 24.9 percent for books and 18.1 percent for periodicals; the Faculty of Oriental Languages and Linguistics has received 4.0 percent for books, and 1.8 percent for periodicals; and the Faculty of Education has received 0.8 percent for books and 0.3 percent for periodicals.

Table 8

Ratio of Books and Periodicals Expenditure in AUL and MKUL

Plan Period	*Faculty of Arts*		*Faculty of S & T*		*Faculty of OL & Linguistics*		*Faculty of Education*		*Total*	
	AUL	*MKUL*	*AUL*	*MKUL*	*AUL*	*MKUL*	*AUL*	*MKUL*	*AUL*	*MKUL*
A	4:1	3:1	2:1	4:1	7:1	3:1	6:1	4:1	3:1	4:1
IV	3:1	3:1	2:1	4:1	3:1	2:1	8:1	4:1	2:1	3:1
V	2.5:1	2:1	1:1	3:1	3:1	2:1	3:1	3:1	2:1	3:1
VI	4:1	1:1	2:1	1:1	3:1	2:1	2:1	3:1	2:1	1:1
VII	3:1	1:1	1:1	1:1	2:1	2:1	2.5:1	2:1	1.5:1	1:1
Total	3:1	2:1	1.5:1	1:1	3:1	2:1	3:1	3:1	2:1	1.5:1

Source: Computed.

The above analysis sheds light on the fact that AUL has given higher priority to the Faculty of S&T in the allotment of funds, while MKUL has given equal preference to the Faculties of Arts, Science and Technology.

Ratio of Books and Periodicals Expenditure

An examination of the ratio of book and periodical expenditure of the different faculties will give further insight into the relative importance attached to each form of materials. The relevant data are given in Table 8.

It may be observed from the table that the ratio of books and periodicals expenditure of AUL on Arts has declined from 4:1 to 2.5:1 till the V plan. It again rises to 4:1 in the VI plan, reflecting the greater demand for book expenditure so as to cater to the rising demands of the students of new courses such as Management studies, Demographic studies, Development studies and Library Science. As against this, the ratio of books and periodical expenditure on Arts in MKUL has narrowed down from 3:1 to 1:1 revealing the emphasis given to research activities in the Faculty of Arts.

In the case of S & T, AUL has maintained the ratio of 2:1 in the successive plan periods except the V and VII, while MKUL has narrowed down from 4:1 to 1:1 over the years, signifying the enhancement of periodical expenditure to support research in the Faculty of S & T.

As against this, the ratio for the Faculties of OL and Linguistics is 3:1 in AUL and 2:1 in MKUL in all the plan periods except the Annual plan. The same trend is identified in the Faculty of Education also.

But one redeeming feature is that generally the ratio of book and periodical expenditure has narrowed down over the years. This is particularly apparent from the V plan onwards, showing the added emphasis given to the periodical subscription

Table 9

Periodical Commitment on Each Rupee Spent on Books

Plan Period	*Faculty of Arts*		*Faculty of S & T*		*Faculty of OL & Linguistics*		*Faculty of Education*		*Total*	
	AUL	*MKUL*	*AUL*	*MKUL*	*AUL*	*MKUL*	*AUL*	*MKUL*	*AUL*	*MKUL*
A	0.26	0.3	0.49	0.23	0.15	0.31	0.17	0.27	0.39	0.27
IV	0.32	0.32	0.6	0.25	0.32	0.44	0.12	0.29	0.42	0.30
V	0.39	0.5	0.89	0.34	0.39	0.66	0.38	0.34	0.72	0.41
VI	0.26	0.75	0.5	0.80	0.33	0.67	0.47	0A0	0.44	0.77
VII	0.35	0.80	0.82	1.1	0.57	0.67	0.40	0.48	0.69	0.91
Total	0.31	0.64	0.64	0.70	0.37	0.60	0.35	0.37	0.55	0.66

Source: Computed.

so as to support the growing research activities in the various Faculties.

Periodical Commitment on each Rupee Spent on Books

An analysis of the periodical expenditure in terms of a rupee spent on books will give a clear understanding of the material expenditure for different Faculties. The relevant data are presented in Table 9.

From the Table it may be observed that, at AUL for each rupee spent on books, Rs. 0.31 was spent for periodicals in the Faculty of Arts, Rs. 0.64 for S & T, Rs. 0.37 for Oriental Languages and Linguistics and Rs. 0.35 for Education.

As against this, in MKUL, for each rupee spent on books, Rs. 0.64 was spent for periodicals in the Faculty of Arts, Rs. 0.70 for S & T, Rs. 0.60 for OL and Linguistics and Rs. 0.37 for Education.

Further in both the libraries, the Faculty of S & T has received relatively larger amount for the subscription of periodicals. It is also interesting to note that comparatively, MKUL has spent higher proportion on periodicals rather than AUL in all the faculties.

But when comparing the book and periodical expenditure with the standards of Koch[3]* and Randall,** both the libraries have come only near to the prescribed standards. The proportion of amount alloted for the subscription of periodicals is to be increased further in order to satisfy fully the given criteria.

An examination of the funds alloted to the Acquisition units of the sample libraries reveals that 90 to 92 percent has

---

* Koch has recommended a Budget Model for Book and periodical expenditure. According to him the ratio of expenditure on periodicals to that on monographs is of 7:k for Universities.

** Randall has also insisted that expenditure on periodicals should be two to three times more than the book costs.

Table 10
Growth of Library Collection in AUL and MKUL

Plan Period	*Total Collections*		*Additions*		*Annual Average Additions*		*Growth Rate of additions*	
	AUL	*MKUL*	*AUL*	*MKUL*	*AUL*	*MKUL*	*AUL*	*MKUL*
A	149535	30622	11715	5982	3905	1994	100	100
IV	174480	56762	24945	26140	4989	5228	128	262
V	207802	100100	33322	44338	6664	8868	171	445
VI	269924	172046	62122	70946	2424	14189	318	712

Source: Computed.

been diverted for acquiring reading materials and the residual to labour and miscellaneous items. The material funds has been shared among the books and periodicals in the ratio of 2:1 in AUL and 3:2 in MKUL. From the funds alloted for books, AUL has spent three-fourths for S & T (71%) and the remaining for Arts (22%) OL & Linguistics (5%) and Education (2%).

As against this, MKUL has allocated its book expenditure in the order of 50.7 percent for Arts, 43 percent for S & T, 5 percent for OL and Linguistics and 1.3 percent for Education over the years. The same pattern is discernible in the allocation of periodical expenditure in both the Libraries.

The allocation pattern of material expenditure may further be analysed by taking into account the development of collection in the sample Libraries.

A rational distribution of the material budget can better be assessed by taking to consideration the development of collection on the basis of the (i) number and diversity of instructionaland research programmes, (ii) users' strength, (iii) introduction of new courses, (iv) requirements of the individual departments, (v) size of the existing collection and (vi) utilisation of the collection. Based on the above mentioned factors, the collection development of the sample libraries has been attempted.

Growth of Library Collection in AUL and MKUL

The total collection of the AUL has increased significantly from 1.49 lakhs volumes in the Annual plan to 3.1 lakhs volumes in the VII plan, recording a 2 fold increase (vide Table 10). As against this, the collection of MKUL has increased from 30,000 volumes to 2.16 lakhs, registering a 7.2 fold increase over the years. During the VI plan period, largest number of volumes were added as a result of higher allotment, thanks to the stress on education and human resource development.

This is reflected in the total addition of nearly 62122 volumes as against 33322 volumes in the previous plan period in AUL. Similarly MKUL has added 70496 volumes in the VI plan as against 44338 volumes in the previous plan periods.

The annual average addition of volumes has grown at a constant rate in AUL marking 1.7 fold increase from 3905 volumes to 6664 volumes till the V plan period and it has doubled only during the VI plan period. As against this, in MKUL the annual average addition of volumes has shown a sharp increase from 1994 volumes to 5228 volumes during the IV plan, recording a three-fold increase, while maintaining a two fold increase of additions in the last three plan periods.

An analysis of the total growth rate over the plan periods given in Table 10, indicates a general rising trend in both the Libraries. The growth rate in AUL during the last three plan periods has, however, shown a rising trend though at a relatively low level. In MKUL, the growth rate has been constant during the successive plan periods. For the whole plan periods, the annual growth works out to be 3.27 percent for AUL and 7.37 percent for MKUL.

Reckoned in terms of the standard of collection, it is interesting to note that growth rate of collections of MKUL has fulfilled the Randall[4]* criteria of 6-10 percent annual additions to the total stock during the last two plan periods. This may be due to the allotment of liberal finance to MKUL consequent on the stress on the human resource development programmes in the Five Year Plans. AUL must be given more allotment to the procurement of books and periodicals inorder to satisfy Randall[5] criteria.

---

* In order to calculate the growth of library collections, the norm suggested by Randall has been adopted. He has recommended that the annual accessions for the libraries should be between six and ten percent of the total number of books in the collection of an established University inorder to keep the collection on the current side of obsolecence.

Growth of Books and Periodicals

Data relating to the growth of books and periodicals are furnished in Table 11. It is apparent from the Table that the book collection in AUL has recorded only 3 fold increase as against 8 fold, increase in MKUL. The growth rate of book collection which was constant till the V plan stepped up considerably during the VI plan, consequent on the introduction of new courses in the Faculties of Arts, Science and Technology. In the case of MKUL, the growth rate has nearly doubled in the successive plan periods. This is explained by the fact that MKUL has concentrated more on strengthening its book collection to meet the instructional programme of the University. The annual average addition of book collection also confirms this. In MKUL, the annual average addition has shown a sharp increase in the IV plan which has almost doubled in V and VI plan. As against this, the annual average additions in AUL has been gradual in all the plan periods except the VI plan, when it has reached the peak of adding 56,862 volumes.

In the case of periodicals, the annual average additions in AUL has increased from 357 in the Annual plan to in the VI plan period by registering 1.3 fold increase over the plan periods. As against this, the annual periodical additions in the MKUL has increased from 150 to 634 recording more than four fold increase over the plan periods. From the V plan onwards the growth rate of periodicals has registered significant increases in both the Libraries. This is meant to meet the growing demands, consequent on the introduction of M.Phil. programmes, increase in the enrollment of M. Phil., Ph.D. scholars and the insistence on the research degree for the staff in both the Universities.

Ratio of Books to Periodicals

The ratio of books to periodicals is an indicator of collection policy. Looked at from this angle, it is interesting to note that in AUL upto V plan the ratio was 7:1 and in the next two plans,

Table 11
Growth of Books and Periodicals

Plan Period	Total Book Collection		Total Periodical Collection		Book Addition		Periodical Additions		Annual Average		Annual Average Periodical Addition		Growth Rate of Books		Growth Rate of Periodicals	
	AUL	MKUL	AUL	MKUL	AUL	MKUL	AUL	MKUL	AUL	MKUL	AUL	MKUL	AUL	MKUL	AUL	MKUL
A	130774	28157	18761	2465	10644	5533	1071	449	3548	1844	357	150	100	100	100	100
IV	153329	52905	21151	3857	22555	24748	2390	1392	4511	4950	478	278	127	268	134	185
V	182406	95054	25396	6046	29077	41149	4245	2190	5815	8430	849	438	164	457	238	292
VI	239268	162873	30656	9173	56862	67819	5260	3127	11372	13564	1052	625	321	736	295	417
VII	273790	205051	34391	11075	34522	42178	3735	1902	11507	14059	1245	634	324	762	349	423

Source: Computed.

Table 12A

Composition of Library Collections Among Faculties

Plan Period	*Faculty of Arts*		*Faculty of S & T*		*Faculty of OL & Linguistics*		*Faculty of Education*	
	AUL	*MKUL*	*AUL*	*MKUL*	*AUL*	*MKUL*	*AUL*	*MKUL*
A	56925	15081	63465	11463	*25751*	3391	3394	687
IV	65945	26849	75840	22798	28441	5774	4254	1341
V	*773Z5*	*ti77S5*	92065	41969	32538	9047	5814	2299
VI	93410	79488	133630	75819	35345	13243	7539	3496
VII	101270	100600	162852	*95000*	36040	16120	8019	4310

Source: Computed.

it was 8:1. As against this in MKUL, the ratio has registered a steep increase from 11:1 to 19:1 over the years, indicating its emphasis on books rather than periodicals to meet the demands arise out of the expansion of courses.

Composition of Library Collections among Faculties

An analysis of the library collections acquired for the various faculties will give a clear insight into the pattern of library collections. The details pertaining to the collections of different faculties are furnished in Table 12A.

In AUL, out of every 100 volumes acquired, 33 belongs to Arts, 52 Sciences, 12 OL and Linguistics and 3 Education. In MKUL, out of every 100 volumes 47 belongs to Arts, H Sciences, 8 OL & Linguistics and 2 Education. The predominance of collection in Arts and Sciences in both the Libraries is explained by the fact that these have been the main courses of study and research over the years. Languages and Linguistics have claimed the next priority followed by Education (vide Table 12B).

The relative rate of growth of collections among the faculties has been analysed in Table 12C. It is interesting to note that in AUL, the Faculties of S & T, OL and Linguistics have recorded more than 2 fold increase while that of Arts and Education have shown an increase of 1.7 times and IA times respectively over the plan periods. The expansion of the courses in S & T from the VI plan period has enabled large inflow of funds, thereby increasing the collection of books. Linguistics being an Advanced Centre has received special grants during V plan. This has resulted in a slight rise in the rate of collection in the Faculty of OL and Linguistics. Though the number of books in the Arts and Education Faculties has shown a rising trend, the rate of growth is very low. This is due to the decrease in the proportion of funds sanctioned to these Faculties, consequent on the introduction of Correspondence Courses and the subsequent fall in enrollment.

Table 12B

Proportion of Library Collection among Faculties

Plan Period	*Faculty of Arts*		*Faculty of S & T*		*Faculty of OL & Linguistics*		*Faculty of Education*	
	AUL	*MKUL*	*AUL*	*MKUL*	*AUL*	*MKUL*	*AUL*	*MKUL*
A	38.0	49.2	42.0	37.4	17.5	11.0	2.5	2.4
IV	37.9	47.3	43.0	40.2	16.7	10.2	2.4	2.3
V	37.4	47.3	44.0	41.5	16.0	8.9	2.6	2.3
VI	35.7	46.2	47.4	44.1	14.1	7.7	2.8	2.0
VII	33.0	46.5	51.8	44.0	12.1	7.5	2.7	2.0

Source: Computed.

Table 12C
Growth Rate of Collection Among Faculties

Plan period	*Faculty of Arts*		*Faculty of S & T*		*Faculty of OL & Linguistics*		*Faculty of Education*		*Total*	
	AUL	*MKUL*	*AUL*	*MKUL*	*AUL*	*MKUL*	*AUL*	*MKUL*	*AUL*	*MKUL*
A	100	100	100	100	100	100	100	100	100	100
IV	116	178	120	199	111	170	125	195	128	262
V	135	317	145	366	126	267	171	335	171	445
VI	164	527	311	661	137	391	222	509	318	712
VII	178	667	257	829	140	475	276	627	327	737

Source: Computed.

As against this, in MKUL, the Faculty of S & T has recorded more than 8 fold increase over the years. The rate of increase is almost doubled in the successive plan periods. Next comes the Faculty of Arts, whose rate of growth is gradual till IV plan but increased sharply (6 fold increase) during the last three plan periods. Similarly, the Faculty of Education has recorded more than 6 fold increase followed by OL and Linguistics which has shown only a 5 fold increase. Comparatively the rate of growth of library collections in the Faculties of MKUL have been higher due to the larger provision of funds.

Performance Evaluation of the Acquisition Unit

The performance of the Acquisition unit can now be evaluated on the basis of the funds received for acquisition and the nature of the collection. The criteria used to measure the performance effectiveness of this unit includes:

(i) Testing the adequacy of the book-budget allocation, (ii) Examining the adequacy of the collection size, (iii) Assessing the optimum size of the library collection and (iv) Measuring the efficiency of the collection.

Testing the Adequacy of the Book Budget[6] Allocation

The adequacy of the book budget allocation is to be assessed in terms of the norms suggested. In this context, the Kothari Commission recommendation (1966) of a sum of Rs. 300 per Faculty member for book purchase is taken as a common norm for all kinds of users. But it has been modified by assigning credit points to each category of users by taking into consideration the degree of their utilisation of the library. As the teachers and research scholars use the library more often than the other categories, they are assigned one credit point; M.Phil. students 0.75 credit points, P.G. students 0.5 points; Graduate students 0.25 credit points. The book norm for each year is then calculated by using the whole sale price Index so as to give allowance for the rise in the price of books.

Funds alloted to the books by the two University Libraries and their position with regard to the above norms are presented in Table 13.

It is revealing to note that the book cost per user of the AUL has recorded a 4.8 fold increase from Rs. 92 in the Annual plan to Rs. 440 in the VII plan, while that of MKUL has registered a 1.5 fold increase from Rs. 1391 to Rs. 2105 over the plan periods. Though the rate of growth has shown a sharp increase in AUL (4.8 fold) in absolute terms, the cost per user of MKUL is significantly greater than that of AUL, and the proportion of variation ranges from 77 percent to 93 percent over the plan periods. This may be attributed to the lumpsum grants received by the MKUL during the study period for the procurement of library materials.

A comparison of the alloted book budget with the norms indicates that AUL has not reached the level suggested and the proportion of variation ranges from 63 percent to 75 percent. This may perhaps due to the inadequate financial support. The magnitude of variation in AUL therefore, need to be redressed by adopting apragmatic allocation policy based on the growth in the user population.

As against this in MKUL, the book budget allocation has far exceeded the norm but the percentage of variation gets declined over the plan periods which may be attributed to the enormous increase in the user population in the last three plan periods.

It is thus evident from the above analysis that the MKUL has received adequate book funds to support the growing enrollment of students and the strength of the staff members, while the opposite trend has prevailed in AUL.

Examining the Adequacy of the Collection Size

The adequacy of the collection size refers to the number of volumes available per student to satisfy his information

Table 13

Testing the Adequacy of the Book-budget Allocation (Rupees)

Plan Period	*Book cost per user*			*Variation*	
	AUL	*MKUL*	*As per norm*	*AUL*	*MKUL*
A		1391	351	-259	+1040
IV	121	1699		-324	+1254
V	179	1277	706	-527	+ 571
VI	382	1646	1039	-657	+ 607
VII	440	2105	1338	-898	+ 767

Source: Computed.

Table 14
Examining the Adequacy of the Collection Size

Plan period	*Collection in AUL (GM)*	*User population in AUL (GM)*	*Ratio*	*Collection in MKUL (GM)*	*User population in MKUL (GM)*	*Ratio*	*Volume per user ratio of AUL & MKUL*	*Comparison of population ratio of AUL & MKUL*
A	145440	4994	29	28330	205	137	1:5	24:1
IV	163963	6249	26	68598	386	178	1:7	16:1
V	193678	7831	25	129297	747	173	1:7	10:1
VI	242383	8173	30	200410	1177	170	1:6	7:1
VII	295123	8645	34	256433	1518	169	1:5	6:1

Source: Computed.

requirement.* In this context, Downs and Heusman[7] have suggested a ratio of 1:100 while Peep and Sinkevicius[8] 1:125. The volume per user of the sample libraries has been examined from this standard. The relevant data are presented in Table 14.

It is interesting to note that the volume per user of the AUL and MKUL has exhibited a mixed trend during the study under review. In AUL, it has shown a decline from 29 volumes to 25 till the V plan period which may be attributed to the rapid increase in the rate of growth of users. But in the last two plan periods, it has shown considerable increase, which may be explained by the receipt of large book grants during the VI and VII plan and the consequent increase in the number of volumes added.

As against this, in MKUL, the volume per user has shown a sharp increase from 137 volumes to 178 till the IV plan. But it declined gradually in the successive plan periods from 173 to169; consequent on the four fold increase in the user population.

But the number of volumes available per student in MKUL is higher than the suggested norm. As against this, AUL has remained far below the suggested norm. This may be explained by the fact that AUL, being a unitary, residential institution has got a large number user population, while MKUL being a affiliated type has lesser number of users. This is supported by the fact that the proportion of users in AUL is 9 times larger than MKUL during the study period.

---

* To measure the adequacy of the library collection the volume per user has been calculated by adopting the following procedure: Collection size Volume per user (ratio) user population.
This ratio has been compared with the standards suggested by Downs and Heusman, Peep and Sinkevicius. The former has recommended 100 volumes per student while the latter has recommended 125 volumes per student.

From the above analysis, it is clear that the number of volumes available per user in MKUL is higher than AUL. Forevery volume available to the user in AUL, the number of volumes available to the user in MKUL ranges from 5 to 7.

Measuring the Optimum Size of the Library Collection

The optimum size of the library collection refers to the number of (relevant) usable items in the collection. This has to be determined by taking in to consideration the use per volume. Stoijarov has suggested 'Loan per volume' and 'Loan per reader as the criteria to judge the relevancy of the collection. According tohim maximum loan/use per volume per year is three and the Minimum is 1.5. This formula may be adopted to calculate the optimum size of the sample libraries, and it is based on the following assumption:

a = the number of laons per volume
b = the number of loans
c = the number of volumes in stock
d = the number of readers
e = the number of loans per reader
f = the number of books per reader

The number of loans per volume equals the total number of loans, divided by the number of volume in stock, or a = b/c

The number of loans and volumes can be expressed in different ways. The number of loans equals the number of readers multiplied by the number of loans per reader, or

B= d x e

These new values are substituted into the original equation to give,

In other words, the number of books per reader equals the number of loans per reader divided by the number of loans per volume:

Table 15A
Measuring the Optimum Size of the Library Collection in AUL

Plan period	*Number of volumes in stock (C)*	*No. of loans (b)*	*Loan per volume (a=b/c)*	*No. of readers (d)*	*No. of loan per reader (c)*	*No. of volumes per reader (f)*	*A=e/f*
A	149535	41584	0.3	4994	8	30	0.3
IV	174480	68598	0.4	6249	11	28	0.4
V	107802	129297	0.6	7831	17	27	0.6
VI	269924	200411	0.7	8173	25	33	0.7
VII	308181	256433	0.9	8645	30	35	0.9

Source: Computed.

Table 15B
Measuring the Optimum Size of the Library Collection in MKUL

Plan period	*Number of volumes in stock (C)*	*No. of loans (b)*	*Loan per volume (a=b / c)*	*No. of readers (d)*	*No. of loan per reader (c)*	*No. of volumes per reader (f)*	*A=e / f*
A	30622	26595	0.9	205	130	149	0.9
IV	56762	54868	0.97	386	142	147	0.97
V	100100	111035	1.1	754	147	132	1.1
VI	172046	188280	1.1	1177	160	146	1.1
VII	216126	253458	1.2	1518	167	142	1.2

Source: Computed.

Stoljarov[9] feels that any attempt to optimise the size of the stock must pay regard to the use per volume, this is infact the measure by which the optimisation of the size is assessed.

The data relevant to the computation of the optimum size of the Library collections are presented in Table 15.

It is interesting to note that the loan per volume has increased from 0.3 to 0.9 in AUL and from 0.9 to in MKUL. From this, it may be inferred that MKUL has satisfied the absolute minimum 'use per volume of one loan a year during the successive plan periods except the Annual plan, while AUL has come only close to this norm. This can be increased by increasing the number of additions in accordance with the need, and updating the stock regularly, thereby keeping the stock ready for use.

Measuring the Efficiency of the Library Collection

Efficiency of the library collection refers to its accessibility and it can be analysed in terms of the rotation (circulation). The efficiency of the collection of the sample libraries has been computed by using the following formula.

M VP (X) - G-M(Y)

Where G.M(Y) and G.M(X.) represent the geometric means of output (circulation) and input (collections) respectively. The a, is the regression coefficient representing elasticities of production with respect to X, (1 to 5). The marginal value of the output is calculated by dividing the geometric mean of 'V by the G.M. of X. From the calculated value, the following results can be obtained. If the calculated value is equal to one, it implies, a constant return from the input; more than one indicating increasing return from the input; less than one diminishing return,* indicating that the input has to be improved.

Analysis of the efficiency of the library collection on the above lines indicates that the MKUL shows an increasing

Table 16
Measuring the Efficiency of the Library Collection (Productivity)

Library	*Collection (X)*	*Circulation (Y)*	*Regression Coefficient (a)*	*Productivity (MVP)*
AUL	200176	115400	0.6795	0.39
MKUL	78010	97659	0.8678	1.86

Source: Computed.

efficiency, while AUL shows a low return. This implies that AUL has to improve its efficiency by incresing and updating the stock (vide Table 16).

Another parameter to measure the efficiency of the library stock is the 'recall value' which is defined as the availability of the documents at the time of demand. In other words, the recall ratio expresses the capability of the stock in meeting the user needs. This has to be calculated by using the following formula suggested by Lancaster[10]. *

Number of Documents Retrieve X= 100

Total Number of Documents is in the % collection. The calculated value as given in Table 17 shows that the recall ratio has increased from 29 to 87 percent in AUL recording a 3 fold increase over the plan periods, while MKUL has registered 1.3 fold increase from 95 percent to137 percent upto the VI plan period. The slight fall (127 percent) in the VII plan may be due to the decrease in the rate of growth of collection during this period.

Though the rate of growth of recall ratio has been higher in AUL, in terms of proportion, MKUL is higher than that of

* It is known that the use of a book decreases with age, and there must be diminishing marginal utility with respect to the range of titles.

Table 17
Measuring the Recall Value of Library Collection

Plan Period	*Total Number of Documents (GM)*		*Documents Retrieved (GM)*		*Recall Ratio in Percentage*	
	AUL	*MKUL*	*AUL*	*MKUL*	*AUL*	*MKUL*
A	145440	28130	41584	26595	29	95
IV	163963	68598	44190	54868	42	124
V	193678	129297	81273	111035	67	137
VI	242384	200410	138990	188280	83	135
VII	295123	256433	198964	253458	87	127

Source: **Computed.**

AULandthe variation ranges from 32 percent to 69 percent. This may be explained by the lack of relevant collection and lack in updating the collection in AUL. This situation needs to be rectified by means of allocating adequate book funds to AUL.

Notes

1. Charles B. Osburn. Academic Research and Library Resources. London: Greenwood Press, 1979, p. 96.

2. Fabian A. Ehikhamenor. "A Formula for Allocating Book Funds: The search for simplicity and Flexibility". Libri, Vol. 33. No. 2, 1983. p. 151.

3. Hans-AlbrechtKoch. "Research on budgeting and standards for academic libraries in the Federal Republic of Germany". Journal of Librarianship,Vol. 17, No. 4, Oct. 1985. p. 272.

4. Gordon E. Randall. "Budgeting for Libraries." Special Libraries, Vol. 67, Jan. 1976. p. 10.

5. *Ibid.*, p. 10.

6. A.K. Guha and P.K. Jayaswal. "Budget Management in Libraries." In: S.K. Kapoor (Ed.) Application of Management Techniques to Library and Information systems. Calcutta: IASLIC, 1979. p. 73.

7. R.B. Downs and J.W. Heusman. "Standards for University Libraries" College and Research Libraries, Vol. 31, No. l, 1970. p. 30.

8. L. Peep and K. Sinkevicius."Financing system of USSR University Libraries". College and Research Libraries, May 1974. p. 180.

9. J.N. Stoljarov. "Optimum size of Public Library stocks". Unesco Bulletin for Libraries, Vol. 27, No. l, Jan-Feb. 1973. p. 42.

10. F. Wilfred Lancaster. Information Retrieval Systems: Characteristics, Testing and Evaluation. New York: John Wiley & Sons, 1979. p. 112.

8

Evaluation of the Performance of the Technical Unit of the AUL and MKUL

The processing unit is an important adjunct of library service. It serves as a significant interface between document acquisition and its accessibility. It also helps to expedite the preparatory work and keep the book ready for use. The organised machinery of the processing unit helps rendering better readers services.

The functions of the processing unit includes classification, cataloguing and physical preparation of library materials for use. In recent years, the increasing material, staff and overhead cost on the one side and the limited finance on the other, force the Librarians to organise and administer the technical activities with utmost economy, efficiency and speed, within the available infrastructure. This has forced them to assess the performance of the various activities of the Technical Unit from the point of view of (i) budget provision, (ii) the availability of personnel and (iii) the return from the unit.

Table 1A
Input Factors of the Processing Units in AUL (Rupees)

Plan period	*Building and furniture cost (GM)*	*Raw Material cost (GM)*	*Binding cost (GM)*	*Labour cost (GM)*	*Miscellaneous (GM)*	*Total (GM)*
	(1)	(2)	(3)	(4)	(5)	(6)
A	4887	1738	5000	19066	1089	31780
IV	4508	3427	7000	29423	1522	45850
V	4077	6339	8000	47915	2432	68763
VI	3682	8972	10000	88831	3598	115083
VII	3398	10992	10000	139717	4746	168851

Source: Computed.

Table 1B

Input Factors of the Processing Units in MKUL (Rupees)

Plan period	*Building and furniture cost (GM)*	*Raw Material cost (GM)*	*Binding cost (GM)*	*Labour cost (GM)*	*Miscellaneous (GM)*	*Total (GM)*
A	5628	1554	3557	25278	605	36622
IV	5203	3436	5908	48283	1805	64680
V	4706	5186	13510	82516	3587	109502
VI	4247	8407	22819	131509	4591	171573
VII	3907	10000	36593	188393	4943	243836

Source: Computed.

Analysis of economy indicates the rational distribution of the budget among the input items such as labour, raw materials, space, furniture and equipment, so as to bring about maximum benefit with least cost. Efficiency depends upon the work of the qualified and high calibre personnel. Speed is to be determined by the contribution of technical services for the readers' services.

Thus, the economy of the processing unit is to be examined in terms of unit cost of the technical services; speed in terms of the number of volumes released and kept ready for use; efficiency in terms of total input and output and identifying the factors which contribute to the efficient functioning of the technical unit.

The Input Factors of the Processing Unit

The processing unit consists of various cost items such as (i) building, (ii) furniture, (iii) D personnel, (iv) raw materials (stationery), (v) binding and (vi) others. An analysis of the input items of the technical unit will throw light on its contribution to the output of the unit. Data pertaining to the distribution of expenditure among the input items of the processing unit in AUL and MKUL are furnished in Table 1.

A cursory glance over the table indicates that personnel account for the biggest junk of the total expenditure on technical services. Expenditure on personnel in AUL has increased from Rs. 0.19 lakhs to Rs. 1.39 lakhs recording a 7.3 fold increase. As against this, in MKUL the share of personnel has increased from Rs. 0.25 lakhs to Rs. 1.85 lakhs registering a 7.5 fold increase. The proportion analysis also confirms this trend. In AUL, the proportion of amount spent on this item has increased from 60 percent to 52.7 percent in MKUL while in AUL it has risen from 69.1 percent to 77.3 percent over the years. In other words, personnel constitutes more than three-fourths of the total expenditure in MKUL, while it has increased from two-thirds to four-fifths in AUL. But in absolute terms, the amount

Table 1C

Proportion Analysis of the Input Factors in AUL

Plan period	*Building and furniture cost (GM)*	*Raw Material cost (GM)*	*Binding cost (GM)*	*Labour cost (GM)*	*Miscellaneous (GM)*	*Total (GM)*
A	15.4	5.5	15.7	60.1	3.1	100
IV	9.8	7.5	15.3	64.1	3.3	100
V	5.9	9.2	11.6	69.7	3.6	100
VI	3.2	7.8	8.7	71.2	3.1	100
VII	2.2	6.5	5.9	82.7	2.9	100

Source: Computed.

Table 1D
Proportion Analysis of the Input Factors in MKUL

Plan period	*Building and furniture cost (GM)*	*Raw Material cost (GM)*	*Binding cost (GM)*	*Labour cost (GM)*	*Miscellaneous (GM)*	*Total (GM)*
A	15.4	4.2	9.7	69.1	1.6	100
IV	8.0	5.3	9.1	74.6	3.0	100
V	4.3	4.7	12.3	75.4	3.3	100
VI	2.5	4.9	13.3	76.7	2.6	100
VII	1.6	4.1	15.0	77.3	2.0	100

Source: Computed.

devoted to personnel in MKUL is higher than in AUL. This is explained by the fact that MKUL, being a Government institution has been provided more to spend on staff salaries, while AUL being a unitary private institution has to manage with less financial provision for staff establishment.

The higher allotment to the personnel in the technical section of the sample libraries is to be attributed to the nature of work which demands more of highly qualified and well trained personnel to attend to classifications, cataloguing, etc.

Next to the personnel, comes binding. In absolute terms, expenditure on binding has doubled over the plan periods from Rs. 5 thousands to Rs. 10 thousands in AUL, while in MKUL it has increased from Rs. 3550 to Rs. 36,590 recording more than 20 fold increase. In terms of proportion the amount spent on binding has declined from 15.7 percent to 5.9 percent in AUL, while the proportion has increased from 9.7 percent to 15 percent in MKUL. In other words the binding in AUL has increased at adiminishing rate. Comparatively, the amount spent on binding in MKUL has been larger at Rs. 82,400 than that of AUL (Rs. 40,000).

Expenditure on stationery has been more or less the same in both the AUL and MKUL. It has increased from Rs. 1735 to Rs. 10992 in AUL recording a 6.3 fold increase over the plan priods while MKUL has risen from Rs.1554 to Rs. 10,000 marking an increase of 6.4 times. But in proportionate terms, it has ranged from 5.5 percent to 9.2 percent in AUL, while in MKUL it has ranged from 4.1 to 5 percent on raw materials. Comparatively both the Libraries have spent equal amount on raw materials.

In absolute terms, the amount spent on building and furniture is relatively higher in MKUL (Rs. 23691) than that of AUL (Rs. 20550). In terms of proportion, both the Libraries have recorded declining trend. This is natural as the cost of building and furniture is a non-recurring item which involves only the maintenance expenditure.

A full picture of the total cost of processing unit in both the libraries is inorder. In AUL, the total input cost of the processing unit has increased gradually from Rs. 0.32 lakhs to Rs. 1.69 lakhs recording a five fold increase. As against this, in MKUL, it has increased from Rs. 0.37 lakhs to Rs. 2.44 lakhs registering more than 6 times increase. Throughout the plan periods, the total processing cost of MKUL has been higher than that of AUL, the proportion of variation ranging from 15 percent to 59 percent. This again is in line with the greater allotment of fund received by the MKUL and hence the greater proportion to the Technical unit.

Output of the Processing Unit

The stage is now set to evaluate the quantum of output from the Technical unit. This is to be done by analysing the (i) number of volumes processed and (ii) the total number of catalogue cards prepared. The relevant data are presented in Table 2. It is heartening to note that the number of volumes processed in AUL has increased from 4,228 volumes in the Annual plan to 20,103 volumes in the VII plan recording 6 % fold increase, while in MKUL, it has increased from 2,041 volumes to 24,445 volumes registering a 12 fold increase. Comparatively, the total number of volumes processed in AUL is higher than that of MKUL, which may be attributed to the efforts taken to clear the back log regularly. It is revealing to note that the numbr of catalogue cards prepared in AUL has increased from 10,200 to 1.2 lakhs marking an increase of 12 times. Comparatively, the total number of catalogue cards prepared by AUL has been larger than that of MKUL and the proportion of variation ranges from 10 percent to 52 percent over the years. This may be due to the constant rise in the number of volumes acquired and the promptness in processing the acquired volumes. While measuring the output of the processing unit in monetary

Table 2A

Output of the Processing Unit in AUL

Plan period	*No. of volumes acquired (GM)*	*No. of volumes processed (GM)*	*Average No. of cards per volume processed (GM)*	*Total cards produced*	*Constant money value per card produced Rs.*	*Total output in monetary terms Rs.*
A	3900	4228	5	21140	0.10	2114
IV	4981	6697	5	33485	0.12	4018
V	6653	10531	5	52655	0.14	7372
VI	12334	19188	5	95940	0.16	5350
VI I	12751	29103	5	145515	0.18	26193

Source: Computed.

Table 2B

Output of the Processing Unit in MKUL

Plan period	*No. of volumes acquired (GM)*	*No. of volumes processed (GM)*	*Average No. of cards per volume processed (GM)*	*Total No. of cards produced*	*Constant money value per card produced Rs.*	*Total output in monetary terms Rs.*
A	1922	2041	5	10205	0.10	1020.5
IV	5129	4473	5	22365	0.12	2683.8
V	8834	9460	5	47300	0.14	6622.0
VI	14014	16300	5	81500	0.16	13040.0
VII	14433	24445	5	122225	0.18	22000.5

Source: Computed.

Table 3A

Index of Total Productivity AUL

Plan period	*Total Input Factors* Rs.*	*Total output factors* Rs.*	*Productivity (3/2) Rs.*	*Total Productivity index**
(1)	(2)	(3)	(4)	(5)
A	31780	2114	0.067	100
IV	45880	4018	0.088	131
V	68763	7372	0.107	160
VI	115083	15350	0.138	199
VII	168851	26193	0.155	231

* The total input factor includes labour, binding, raw materials, building and furniture.

* The output factor includes the number of titles processed or the number of cards produced, and the total output is converted into monetary terms.

* The index of total productivity is equal to the current year production divided by the base year production multiplied by 100.

Table 3A
Index of Total Productivity MKUL

Plan period	*Total Input Factors* Rs.*	*Total output factors* Rs.*	*Productivity (3/2) Rs.*	*Total Productivity index**
(1)	(2)	(3)	(4)	(5)
A	36622	1020.5	0.028	100
IV	64680	2683.8	0.041	146
V	109502	6622.0	0.060	214
VI	171573	13040.0	0.076	271
VII	243836	22000.5	0.090	321

terms, it is found that both the Libraries exhibit a rising trend. In AUL, the output has increased from Rs. 2,114 to 26,193 recording a 12.4 fold increase, while in MKUL it has increased from Rs. 1,020 to Rs. 22,000 registering a 22 fold increase over the plan periods. The relatively larger output from the Technical Unit of AUL may again be attributed to its quick and efficient functioning.

Total Productivity of the Technical Unit

Total productivity* is a measure of the efficiency with which the factors input into the Technical Unit are utilised to bring out maximum output. Data relevant to the total productivity of the Technical Unit of the two Libraries are presented in Table 3.

It is clear from the table that there is an upward trend in the total productivity of the processing unit in the sample Libraries. In AUL, it has registered a 2.3 fold increase from Rs. 0.67 to Rs. 0.155. As against this, in MKUL, the productivity has recorded a 3 fold increase from Rs. 0.28 to Rs. 0.90. Totally,

---

* Waldhart and Marcum have given a formula to compute the productivity of economy of the processing unit. The formula is given below:

$$Pt = \frac{Qt}{L+C+R+Q}$$

Where,

Pt = Total Productivity,
L = Labour input factor
C = Capital input factor
R = Raw materials
Q = Miscellaneous items
Qt = Total output

Productivity refers to a comparison of the quantity of products and services produced by an organization and the quantity of resources employed in the production process. Productivity may be expressed as a ratio between output and input.

Sources : S. Fabricant. A Primer on Productivity, Newyork : Random House, 1968.

Table 4
Unit Cost of Processing in AUL and MKUL

Total Technical Processing Cost		*No. of Volumes Processed*		*Unit cost of Processing*	
AUL *Rs.*	*MKUL* *Rs.*	*AUL*	*MKUL*	*AUL* *Rs.*	*MKUL* *Rs.*
25804	30389	4228	2041	6.11	14.88
59850	57627	6697	4473	5.96	12.88
62254	101209	10531	9460	5.88	10.69
107803	162735	19188	16300	5.63	9.98
160709	234986	29103	24445	3.52	9.61
396420	586946	69747	56719	5.68	10.30

the productivity of AUL is larger than that of MKUL which may be explained by the efficient utilisation of there sources.

Unit Cost of the Technical Services

To find out the effectiveness of the processing activities, the unit cost of the technical processing is to be analysed. This will indicate the cost per item processed. Lower the unit cost, higher, is the effectiveness. The unit cost of the technical services is to be computed by dividing the total processing cost by the total volumes processed. While computing the processing cost the items to be taken into account include (i) Labour cost involved in classification and cataloguing; (ii) Stationary cost and (iii) Binding cost. The data relating to the unit cost of the technical services of the Libraries are given in Table 4.

It is interesting to note that in AUL, the cost per unit of processing has decreased from Rs. 6.11 in the Annual plan to Rs. 5.68 in the VII plan. As against this, in MKUL, it has declined from Rs. 14.88 to Rs. 9.61 over the plan periods. Comparatively, the unit cost of AUL is lesser than that of MKUL. This perhaps indicates the efficient functioning of the Technical unit of AUL which results in the relatively larger number of volumes processed within the amount allotted for processing.

The cost per unit of processing in AUL is Rs. 5.68 while that of MKUL is double the amount Rs.10.3. But one significant trend is that both the Libraries have tried to minimise the unit cost over the plan period.

Factors Contributing to the Minimum Unit Cost

The minimisation of the unit cost depends not only on the number of volumes processed, but also on the number of books acquired and working hours. To determine the effect of these three independent variables (X) on the unit cost of processing (Y), multiple linear regression is applied.* The results are presented in Table 5.

Table 5A
Factors Influencing the Unit Cost of Processing in AUL

	No. of books accessioned X_1	*Total working hours* X_2	*Total volumes processed* X_3
Coeifficient	0.1709	0.6809	0.3066
Constant	0.5475	-	-
R-squared	0.9572	-	-
Partial-Correlation	0.0033	0.5183	0.0008

Table 5B

Factors Influencing the Unit Cost of Processing in MKUL

	No. of books accessioned X_1	*Total working hours* X_2	*Total volumes processed* X_3
Coeifficient	1.2423	0.2172	2.2897
Constant	2.9933	-	-
R-squared	0.9585	-	-
Partial-Correlation	0.0846	0.0377	0.1979

The value of 'R' at 0.9572 in AUL and 0.9585 in MKUL is proved to be statistically significant by the value of 'F' statistics which is 126.679 in AUL and 130.954 in MKUL. The positive sign for the co-efficient of all the explanatory variables indicates the good fit of the estimated equation for the unit cost of processing (Y). The fitted equation explains that the above mentioned factors have influenced the unit cost of processing by 96 percent and the remaining part of the variation is due to random variation in unit cost (k%). There is no serious omissions of any explanatory variable or due to error of approximation of functional forms to be log-linear.

An analysis of the effect of each one of the independent variables on unit cost of processing reveals that the number of volumes processed (X) has significant effect (0.1917) followed

* The regression equation is given below:

Y = a + B.X,+ BJ<$_7$ + B-X^, where 'a' is constant;

B, B_B^are co-efficient of determinations;

X, X, X- are independent variables and Y is the dependent variable by the number of books acquired (0.0846) and The total working hours (0.0377) in MKUL. In the case of AUL, the total working hours (0.5183) has contributed largely to the minimum unit cost followed by number of books accessioned (0.0053) and the total volumes processed (0.0008).

It is, thus, clear that all the three variables given above have influenced the unit cost of processing to a great degree (96%) though the individual effect of these factors is found to different in the two Libraries.

Impact of Technical Services on Transaction

The effectiveness of the technical service may also be assessed by analysing the extent of its contribution to the reader's services. In order to compute the impact of the technical

Table 6A

Impact of Technical Services of Library Transaction in AUL

Plan Period	*Circulation* Y	*No. of books processed* X
A	41583	4228
IV	68598	6697
V	12997	10531
VI	200410	19188
VII	256433	29103
Total	696321	29103

Y= 2.19 *+ 0.71* X (0.187)(0.14)

(Numbers in Paranthesis indicate standard errors)

R^2 = 0.57

t_a = 11.71

t_b = 5.67

F = 25.19

* Significance at 1% level.

Table 6B

Impact of Technical Services of Library Transaction in MKUL

Plan Period	*Total Circulation (GM)* Y	*No. of books processed (GM)* X
A	26595	2041
IV	54868	4473
V	111035	9460
VI	188280	16300
VII	253458	24445
Total	634236	56719

Y= 1.36 *+ 0.92* X (0.028) (0.014)

(Numbers in Paranthesis indicate standard errors)

R^2 = 0.99

t_a = 48.57

t_b = 65.71

F = 1881

* Significance at 1% level.

services on transaction (circulation), a linear regression model is applied,* taking circulation as the dependent variable and the number of volumes pr ocessed as the explanatory variable. From the calculated Ic value, the percentage influence of the number of volumes processed (X) on circulation (Y) can be assessed. The result of regression of books processed on circulation is given in Table 6.

It is interesting to note that the value of coefficient of (b) books processed in AUL is 0.71 which is found to be significant (ta cal .> ta tab) at one percent level. This implies that out 2 of 100 books processed, 71 books have been circulated. The R value of AUL (0.57) explains that the number of books processed has influenced the circulation by 57 percent. The 'F' test also 2 confirms that the value of R is statistically significant.

In the same way, in MKUL, the value of 'b' (coefficient of number of books processed) is 0.92, significant at one percent 2 level. The value of R is also highly significant, indicating that the number of volumes processed has influenced circulation by 99 percent.

It is, thus clear that, the processing service greatly influenced the Library performance in both the libraries. Comparatively, the technical service of MKUL is found to be more expeditious resulting in a larger circulation (99%) than that of AUL (57%).

---

* The linear regression model is given below:
Where 'a' is constant; 'b' is co-efficient of determination; 'X' is the independent variable (books processed) and 'Y' is the dependent variable (circulation).

9

Evaluation of the Service Units in AUL and MKUL

The activites of the Service Unit centres around two major services viz., (l) Circulation service and (2) Reference service The circulation service includes (i) lending and return transaction, (ii) reservation, (iii) recall and (iv) reminder routines. The reference service includes (i) directional, (ii) ready reference, (iii) long-range reference, (iv) instructional, (v) reader's advisory and (vi) referral. A proper organisation and administration of these services lead to better utilisation of the library materials as the activities of the service unit are directly related with the readers. Establishment of such a service unit depends on such factors as, (i) adequate number of qualified persons, (ii) sufficient physical facilities viz., spacious reading hall, comfortable furniture and equipment. The performance of this unit has therefore, to be assessed by taking into account the (i) cost factors and (ii) service factors. The cost factors include expenditure in terms of space, furniture, equipment and labour. The service factors include (i) the number of documents circulated, (ii) number of borrowers registered and (iii) number of reference queries answered.

Table 1A
Cost Structure of the Service Unit in AUL

Plan period	*Space cost*	*Furniture cost*	*Labour cost*	*Miscellaneous cost*	*Total service unit cost*
A	10363	4299	10462	1089	26213
	(100)	(100)	(100)	(100)	(100)
IV	9554	3970	14365	1522	29411
	(92.0)	(92.0)	(137)	(139)	(112)
V	8636	3587	26145	2432	40800
	(83.0)	(83.0)	(250)	(223)	(156)
VI	7809	3235	51110	3598	65752
	(75.)	(75.0)	(489)	(330)	(250)
VI I	71S0	2987	82632	4746	97547
	(69.0)	(70.0)	(790)	(436)	(372)
Total	43542	[&0Z0	184714	13387	259723

(Figures in paranthesis represent proportions)

Source: Computed.

Table 1B
Cost Structure of the Service Unit in MKUL

Plan Period	Space cost Rs.	Furniture cost Rs.	Labour cost Rs.	Miscellaneous cost Rs.	Total service unit cost Rs.
A	13698	3190	19597	605	37090
	(100)	(100)	(100)	(100)	(100)
IV	12663	2945	30925	1851	48384
	(92)	(92)	(158)	(306)	(130)
V		2670	53387	3587	71092
	(84)	(84)	(272)	(593)	(192)
VI	10340	2399	92680	4589	110008
	(75)	(75)	(473)	(759)	(297)
VII	9549	2210	147065	4946	163770
	(70)	(69)	(750)	(818)	(442)
Total	57698	13414	343654	15574	430344

(Figures in paranthesis represent proportions)

Source: Computed.

Data relating to the cost structure of the service unit of the sample libraries are presented in Table 1.

A look into the table reveals that the service cost of AUL has recorded an increase of 3.7 times, as against 4.4 times increase in MKUL. During the study period, the expenditure on service unit has increased from Rs. 0.26 lakhs to Rs. 0.97 lakhs, in the AUL and from Rs. 0.37 lakhs to Rs. 1.64 lakhs in the MKUL. Totally, MKUL has spent Rs. 4.3 lakhs on the service unit while AUL spent only Rs. 2.59 lakhs. Thus the amount spent on service unit by MKUL has been higher than AUL and the amount of variation is Rs. 1.7 lakhs over the plan periods.

Of the total cost, a lion's share has been taken by the labour. In the case of AUL, it has increased from Rs. 0.10 lakhs to Rs. 0.82 lakhs, registering an 8 fold increase, while that of MKUL has increased from Rs. 0.20 lakhs to Rs. 1.5 lakhs registering a 7.5 fold increase.

The proportion analysis also has exhibited the same trend. There was a sharp increase in the labour cost in both the libraries. Its share has increased from 40 percent to 84.7 percent in AUL and from 52.8 percent to 89.5 percent in MKUL over the plan periods. Under the different plan periods, the amount alloted for the labour has increased from nearly half of the total cost to four-fifths.

The reason for this larger financial commitment is not difficult to comprehend. The efficient functioning of the service unit depends mostly on the quantum and quality of the labour force employed in this unit, which in turn demands higher allotment on labour. *

* The personnel costs are among the highest of ail the factors making up the total costs of any operational unit. During recent years, budgets have continued to spiral upwards and the staff overhead costs have risen out of proportion to impact on services performed.

Table 1C

Proportion Analysis of Service Unit Cost in AUL

Plan period	*Space cost* %	*Furniture cost* %	*Labour cost* %	*Miscellaneous cost* %	*Total cost* %
A	39.5	16.4	W).0	4.1	100
IV	32.5	13.5	49.0	5.0	100
V	21.2	8.8	64.0	6.0	100
VI	11.9	4.9	11.1	5.5	100
VII	7.4	3.1	84.7	4.8	100

Table 1D
Proportion Analysis of Service Unit Cost in MKUL

Plan Period	*Space cost %*	*Furniture cost %*	*Labour cost %*	*Miscellaneous cost %*	*Total cost %*
A	36.9	8.6	52.8	1.7	100
IV	26.2	6.1	63.9	3.8	100
V	16.1	3.8	75.1	5.0	100
VI	9.4	2.2	84.2	4.2	100
VII	5.8	1.3	89.8	3.1	100

Cost of space comes next, accounting for 13.5 to 16.7 percent of the total service cost. In absolute terms, the amount spent on space has declined from Rs. 10,000 to Rs. 7,000 in AUL and from Rs. 14,000 to Rs. 9,500 in MKUL during the period under review. In terms of proportion, one could also find the same trend. The gradual decline in space cost is explained by the law of indivisibility.*

Similarly, a substantial decline is found in the furniture cost of the service unit. In absolute terms, furniture cost of AUL has recorded decreases from Rs. 4,000 to 3,000 and the rate of decline is 25 percent while in MKUL it has fallen from Rs. 3,000 to Rs. 2,200 and the rate of fall is 27 per cent. The proportion analysis also confirms this trend. In the case of AUL, the proportion of furniture cost declined from 16.4 percent to 8.6 percent, while that of MKUL recorded sharp decline from 5.6 percent to 1.4 percent.

The cause for the decline in the furniture cost is due to the fact that only the depreciation value has been taken into account in the calculation.

As against this, the amount spent on miscellaneous items such as electricity and maintenance have been increasing steadily, from Rs. 1000 to Rs. 4700 recording a 4.1 fold increase in AUL, andfrom Rs. 605 to Rs. 900 registering an 8 fold increase in MKUL:

---

* Because of the indivisible nature of items like building furniture and equipment they have to be erected in one instalment. But as time passes by, their cost spread over the period of time and the cost per unit of time goes on decreasing.

Source: Ahmed H. Helal. "Approaches to the Evaluation of Technical Services in Libraries". In: Lancaster, F.W. and Cleverdon, C.W. Eds. Evaluation and Scientific Management of Libraries and Information Centres, Noordhoff-Leydon, 1977. pp. 101-130.

A. Tejomurty. Studies In Academic Librarianshlp. Jaipur: Printwell, 1987. p. 91.

Looked at from the point of recurring and non-recurring cost, it is interesting to note that both the libraries have spent higher proportions of the total service cost on recurring items and lower percentage on non-recurring items. This is in confirmity with the general trend in the allotment of funds.

Unit Cost of Service

The performance efficiency of the service unit is to be ascertained in terms of unit cost of each services. The most efficient services are those which are achieved with the least cost. Cost per service is calculated by dividing the total cost of the service unit by the total number of service performed in a particular period of time, viz., total number of documents circulated and the total number of reference questions answered etc.

In the light of the above approach, the service units of AUL and MKUL can be assessed by taking into account the unit cost of their services. The relevant data are presented in Table 2.

It is striking to note that the number of outputs in both the libraries have recorded a more than six fold increase during the plan periods. The circulation figure of AUL has shown a steady increase from 0.41 lakhs to 2.56 lakhs recording a 6.2 fold increase, while that of MKUL has increased from 0.27 lakhs to 2.53 lakhs registering a 9.5 fold increase over the years.

Though the output gets increased, the performance efficiency is measured only in terms of providing maximum service atleast cost. Therefore, the cost per unit of service offered by the sample libraries have been calculated.

It is revealing to note that the unit cost of circulation has declined substantially during the study period in both the libraries. It has registered a fall of 40 percent in AUL, ranging from Rs. 0.63 in the annual plan to Rs. 0.38 in the VII plan. As

Table 2A

Unit Cost of Services in AUL

Plan period	*Total number of circulation**	*Total number of queries answered**	*Total service cost* Rs*	*Unit cost per circulation Rs.*	*Unit cost per queries answered Rs.*
A	41584	61820	26213	0.63	
IV	68598	93669	29411	0.42	0.31
V	129297	132287	40800	0.32	0.30
IV	200411	219326	65752	0.32	0.29
VII	256433	329910	97547	0.38	0.29

* Geometric mean.

Table 2B

Unit Cost of Services in MKUL

Plan period	*Total number of Circulation (GM)*	*Total number of queries Answered (GM)*	*Total service Cost (GM) Rs*	*Unit cost per circulation Rs*	*Unit cost per queries answered Rs*
A	26595	26907	37090	104	1.38
IV	54868	56353	48384	0.88	0.85
V	111035	101606	71092	0.64	0.70
IV	188280	166627	110008	0.58	0.66
VII	253458	250580	163770	0.65	0.65

against this in MKUL, the unit cost has marked 54 percent decline, ranging from Rs. 1.4 to Rs. 0.65 over the plan period.

But, comparing the performance of AUL and MKUL, the functioning of AUL has been found to be relatively more efficient than MKUL, as the unit cost of service of AUL is less at Rs. 0.37 than Rs. 0.68 in MKUL. This reflects the efficient arrangement of the service unit in the AUL. AUL being an established University is able to achieve a better performance.

Similarly, the output of reference (number of reference queries answered) has shown impressive record over the plan periods. It has increased from 0.62 lakhs to 3.3 lakhs marking a 5.3 fold increase in AUL, while in MKUL, it has increased from 0.27 lakhs to 2.5 lakhs registering a 9.3 fold increase.

Consequently, the unit cost per reference queries answered has declined steadily. In AUL, the cost per service has declined by 30 percent from Rs. 0.42 in the Annual plan period to Rs. 0.29 in the VII plan, while in MKUL, the decrease is from Rs. 1.38 to Rs. 0.65 recording a decline of 53 percent.

Thus, the cost per unit of reference question answered in AUL is lesser than MKUL signifying the efficient functioning of the Service Unit of AUL. This is due to the larger number of requests made at the 'Reference Desk' which, in turn, reflects the relatively larger number of user population in AUL than that of MKUL.

Marginal Analysis of Costs and Services

The benefits of unit cost will be maximum when the additional increment of outputs and additional increment of cost are equal. This is due to the cost that any other point, either additional revenue could be obtained at less additional cost, or additional revenue obtained would be less than the additional cost incurred.*

---

* Hand book of Economic Analysis. Newyork, Research and Education Association, 1982. pp. G-16.

Table 3A
Marginal Analysis of Costs and Services in AUL

Plan Period	*Marginal cost of service unit (MC) Rs.*	*Marginal benefit from circulation (MB)*	*Marginal benefit from reference (MB)*	*Benefit-cost service unit Circulation*	*ratio of MB/MC Reference*
A	1213	10584	22400	8.7	18.5
IV	3198	27011	31849	8.4	10.0
V	1 1389	60702	38618	5.3	3.4
VI	36341	71 114	87039	2.0	2.4
VI I	31795	56022	110584	1 .8	3.5
Total	83936	225433	290490	2.7	*3.5*

Table 3B

Marginal Analysis of Costs and Services in AUL

Plan Period	*Marginal cost of service unit (MC) Rs.*	*Marginal benefit from circulation (MB)*	*Marginal benefit from reference (MB)*	*Benefit-cost ratio of service unit MB/MC Circulation*	*Reference*
A		22000	21000	2.5	2.7
IV	11294	28273	29446	2.5	2.6
V	22708	56167	45253	2.5	2.0
VI	38916	77245	65021	2.0	1.7
VII	53762	65178	83953	1.2	1.6

An attempt has been made to find out whether the additional expenditure made on the Service Unit has brought about a proportionate additional output. The relevant data are given in Table 3.

It is striking to note that the marginal cost (additional cost) of circulation in AUL has increased from Rs. 1200 to Rs. 31800 recording a 26 fold increase while in MKUL, it has increased from Rs. 8,000 to Rs. 53,800 registering a 6.7 fold increase. As against this, the marginal benefit (additional benefit) of circulation in AUL has increased from 10,600 to 25,600 recording a 5.3 fold increase, while in MKUL, it has increased from 22,000 to 65,200, marking a three fold increase. This indicates that with the increase in the marginal cost service efficiency has also increased.

In order to measure the effect of additional cost on the additional benefit, the benefit-cost ratio* has been calculated by dividing the MB by MC. The result shows that throughout the study period, the BCR is greater than one, which implies that additional circulation output obtained is more than the additional cost incurred in AUL and MKUL.

In the same way, the BCR of reference queries answered is also found to be more than one, signifying that the additional reference output of both the libraries are higher than the additional cost.

Performance Efficiency of the Service Unit in AUL and MKUL

The total performance efficiency** of the servive unit % is measured by taking into account the cost input and service output, accruing from this unit. The major outputs of the service

* To measure the Benefit Cost Ratio (BCR) of the Service Unit, the marginal analysis of the cost and services have been attempted. The procedure is given below:

$$BCR = \frac{\text{Marginal Benefit}}{\text{Marginal Cost}}$$

** Lipetz has suggested a formula to measure the performance efficiency of the Service Unit. The formula is given below:

Table 4
Performance of Service Unit in AUL and MKUL

Plan period	*Total Services (O)*		*Cost of Services (1) Rs*		*Efficiency (E) (O/I)*	
	AUL	*MKUL*	*AUL*	*MKUL*	*AUL*	*MKUL*
A	103404	53502	26213	37090	3.9	1.4
IV	162264	111221	29411	48384	5.5	2.3
V	261584	212641	40800	71092	6.4	3.0
VI	419737	354907	65752	110008	6.4	3.2
VII	586343	504038	97547	163770	6.0	3.1
Total	1533332	1236309	259723	430344	5.9	2.9

units of the sample libraries are circulation and reference. The efficiency of the service unit is to be calculated by dividing the total output by the total service cost incurred in this unit. The relevant data are given in Table 4.

The cost involved in the service unit of AUL has shown a steady increase from Rs. 0.2.5 lakhs to Rs. 0.98 lakhs recording nearly a four fold increase over the plan periods. As against this, MKUL has registered a 4.4 fold increase from Rs. 0.37 lakhs in the Annual plan periods to Rs. 1.63 lakhs in the VII plan periods. Regarding outputs, AUL has shown a sharp increase from 1 lakhs to 5.9 lakhs marking nearly a six fold increase as against MKUL, which has exhibited a substantial increase from 0.5 lakhs to 5 lakhs, showing 9.4 times increase.

The steady growth in the service cost and the number of outputs indicates a significant increase in the efficiency of the service unit in both the Libraries. The 'E' value* of AUL has been increasing from 3.9 in the Annual plan period to 6*A* in the VI plan period recording nearly a 2 fold increase. Similarly, in MKUL, the 'E' value has increased from 1.4 to 3.2 registering 2.3 times increase over the plan periods.

This increase in the 'E' value of the Service unit of the AUL implies that AUL is able to render efficient service than MKUL with the existing manpower and funding levels.

A measure to identify the 'total performance of the Library is by calculating the maximum exposure of individuals (in the

---

$$\text{Performance Efficiency} = \frac{\text{User Result or Service}}{\text{Cost Involved}}$$

The cost factor includes expenditure in terms of materials, personnel, supplies and equipment. The service factor includes the outputs of the Service Units such as Circulation and Reference Service.

* 'E' value indicates Performance Efficiency

Table 5A
Growth in the Performance of the AUL

Plan Period	*Circulation (C) (GM)*	*Visitors (V) (GM)*	*Average exposure per issue $\bar{e}_1$ (days)*	*Average exposure Time per visit ($\bar{e}_2$) (days)*	*Total document exposure time (E) = ($C x \bar{e}_1$) + ($V x \bar{e}_2$) (GM)*	*Population (N) (GM)*	*Performance P=E/N (GM)*
A	41584	61820	7	0.5	321998	4944	65.13
IV	68598	93669	7	0.5	527021	6249	84.34
V	129297	132287	7	0.5	971223	7831	124.02
VI	200411	219320	7	0.5	1512540	8184	184.82
VII	256433	329910	7	0.5	1959986	8645	226.72

Table 5B
Growth in the Performance of the MKUL

Plan Period	*Circulation (C) (GM)*	*Visitors (V) (GM)*	*Average exposure per issue $\bar{e}_1$ (days)*	*Average exposure Time per visit ($\bar{e}_2$) (days)*	*Total document exposure time (E) = ($C x e_1$)+ ($V x e_2$) (GM)*	*Population (N) (GM)*	*Performance P=E / N (GM)*
A	25595	26907	7	0.5	199619	205	974
IV	54868	56353	7	0.5	412253	386	1068
V	111035	101606	7	0.5	828048	747	1108
VI	188280	166627	7	0.5	1401274	1177	1191
VII	253458	250580	7	0.5	1899496	1518	1251

service population) to documents of recorded information.* The total document exposure hours/days has been calculated by taking into consideration the (i) total number of circulation, (ii) total number of visits to the library and (iii) average exposure times (days/hours), per issue and per visit respectively. The performance level of the sample libraries has been computed by dividing the total document exposure hours/days by the total population of the Libraries. The relevant data are given in Table 5.

It is interesting to note that the total performance of the AUL has increased rapidly from 65 to 227 registering an increase of 3.5 times during the period under review. As against this, in MKUL, it has increased from 974 to 1254 registering an increase

Table 6A
Factors Influencing the Library Output
(partial correlation analysis)

Explanatory Variables	*Dependent variable (X_0)*	
	AUL	*MKUL*
X_1 Total expenditure	0.0682	0.0128
X_2 Collection size	0.1152	0.1632
X_3 User population	0.5414	0.7474

* In order to measure the maximum exposure of individuals (in the Service Population) to documents of recorded information Hamburg's model has been adopted. The model is given below:

P = Library performance for the year

E = Total document exposure hours/clays

N = Population of the community served and

E = $(C \times e_1) + (V \times e_2)$, where

C = Total number of circulations

V = Total number of visits to the library

e_1, e_2 = Average exposure times per issue and per visit respectively

of 1.3 times. This may be attributedto the rapid increase in the total document exposure times in both the Libraries, which has increased from 3.2 lakhs to 19.6 lakhs recording an increase of 6.1 times in AUL, andfrom 2 1akhs to 18.9 1akhs registering an increase of 9.5 times in MKUL over the plan period. In addition,* the significant growth in the number of user population has also contributed to the increase in the performance of the sample libraries. In AUL, it has increased from 4944 to 8645 making an increase of 1.7 times, while, in MKUL, it has increased from 974 to 1251 recording an increase of 1.3 times. Comparatively, AUL has exhibited an impressive record than MKUL both in (i) total document exposure times and (ii) total user population. However, the performance ratio of MKUL is higher than that of AUL.

Having seen the performance of the different sections of the library, it is imperative to analyse the total performance in terms of (i) total amount spent on the library, (ii) total collection and (iii) total user population. To find out the variables which

Table 6B

Multiple Linear Regression Analysis
Dependent variable (X_0) = Circulation

Explanatory Variable	*Coefficient of Variable*	
	AUL	*MKUL*
X_1 Total expenditure	0.2598	0.0481
X_2 Collection size	0.9675	0.3162
X_3 User population	1.1717	0.8727
R^2	0.97	0.99

* The log-linear regression model (Cobb-Douglas model) is given below: Log X = alog X.,-niblog X- + clog X, where

X = Circulation;

X = Collectionsize;

^| = Total amount spent on the

X^= User population Library;

have contributed to the total output performance, the log-linear regression model* has been adopted. The results of the regression analysis are presented in Table 6.

It is revealing to note that the user population has influenced the output of the AUL by 54 percent and MKUL 75 percent. Next comes the total collection which has influenced the output by 12 percent in AUL and 16 percent in MKUL. The influence of the total amount spent on the output is found to be very little in both the libraries.

Thus, it is clear from the analysis that among the given variables, the user population has contributed largely to the increasing output, followed by the growth in the collection size. This implies that the turnover from the library can be improved by increasing the library members and the collection size. In order to identify the combined effect of all these input factors on the output, multiple Linear regression model is adopted and the results are given in Table 6.

The value of co-efficient of User population (X) in both the libraries are found to be highly significant at one percent level. This is confirmed by 't' value also. From the value of coefficient of determination (R), it may be inferred that all these three variables have influenced the total output (circulation) to a great extent i.e. 97 percent in AUL and 99 percent in MKUL which are statistically significant.

Notes

1. Ben-Ami Lipetz."The Evaluation of Communication Systems: Some Thought son Effectiveness" *Scitech. News,* Winter 1966. p. 110.

2. Morris Hamburg et al. *Library Planning and Decision-Making Systems.* Cambridge, MA: M.I.T. Press, 1974. p. 274.

10

Findings and Conclusions

(1) An analysis of the financial provision to the sample libraries as shown in Table 1, in Chapter-5 indicates that the MKUL has received larger financial assistance from all sources (inclusive of the UGC grants and the University allotment) than the AUL.Totally, MKUL has received a lumpsum grant of Rs. 247 lakhs while that of AUL Rs.176 lakhs. This is, in tune, with the general guidelines of the UGC and other experts that the newly established libraries must be provided with more funds as they have to grow from the scratch.

(2) An examination of the sources of finance to the sample libraries shown in Table 2A in Chapter 5 indicates that MKUL has received a major portion of its finance from the University funds (65%) followed by UGC (34%) as a total over the years (1967-87). Miscellaneous sources account for only 1%. As against this, AUL has received its funds in the order of 50.7 percent from the UGC, ^7.7 percent from the University funds and 1.6 percent from other sources during the plan periods. While the provision

of University funds has shown a normal rising trend from 56 percent to 72 percent in MKUL over the years, the financial support from the UGC to AUL has shown a sharp increase from 38 percent to 57 percent.

(3) The recurring and non-recurring grants of the sample (1) libraries (vide Table 4A in Chapter V) exhibit a paradoxical trend. While the recurring grants have shown a rising trend, the opposite is true in the case of nonrecurring grants in both the libraries during the study period. The total recurring grants of MKUL is higher (Rs. 242.5 lakhs) than that of AUL (Rs. 171.6 lakhs) over the years (1967-87). But in the case of non-recurring grants, both the libraries have received more or less the same amount (Rs. 4.3 lakhs in AUL and Rs. 5 lakhs in MKUL).

(4) An analysis of the recurring items of expenditure presented in Table 6 in Chapter 5 reveals that a major chunk of the allotted funds viz: 77.8 percent has been spent on reading materials; 19.5 percent on staff salaries and 2.7 percent on the miscellaneous items in both the libraries. But in view of the growing demands for various library services, there is a case for a larger percentage of the recurring grants to be allotted in the future towards staff salaries in both the libraries.

(5) The application of the standard measure of the financial adequacy of the sample libraries presented in Table 7 in Chapter 5 indicates that the per capita expenditure of MKUL has exceeded the suggested norm, while AUL has yet to attain the norm as the users' strength of AUL is much above than that of MKUL in relation to the allotment of funds. In order to improve the cost per user ratio in AUL, the grants received may have to been hanced by taking into account the total strength of users, as expected and in line with the norms observed by libraries in India and abroad.

(6) An analysis of the distribution of funds among the functional units brings to light the fact that the Acquisition unit has consumed four-fifths of the total and the rest has been shared by the other two units viz: Technical unit and Service unit. During the past two decades (1967-87), AUL has spent Rs. 1.47 crores (83.9%) on the Acquisition unit; Rs. 17.65 lakhs (10%) on the Technical unit; and Rs. 10.62 lakhs (6.1%) on the Service unit, while MKUL has spent Rs. 2 crores (82.3%) on the Acquisition unit; Rs. 25.9 lakhs (10.5%) on the Technical unit and Rs. 17.6 lakhs (7.2%) on the Service unit. The allotment of funds by the MKUL to these units is higher than that of AUL. This may be due to the receipt of larger funds from the State Government, and the need to establish the library service from the base (as it being a newly established University). The greater allotment to the Acquisition unit in both the libraries is justified on the basis of growing academic programmes, larger enrollment of students and increase in research activities (vide Table 1A in Chapter 6).

(7) The cost components of the Acquisition unit indicates that both the libraries have spent during the study period, a larger proportion of their funds (90% in AUL and 92.4% in MKUL) on acquisition which is as per norms for libraries in general. This is also found to be in the right direction as the entire library service depends on its collection (vide Table 2 in Chapter 7).

(8) An analysis of the material expenditure reveals that three-fifths have been spent on the procurement of books and the residual two-fifths on the subscription of periodicals (vide Table 3A in Chapter 7). However, the rate of growth of expenditure on periodicals is faster (22 fold in MKUL and 14.5 fold in AUL) than the expenditure on books (8 fold) in both the libraries. The growth rate of periodical expenditure takes a momentum since the 5 plan,

consequent on the greater accent given to research activities in both the Universities (vide Table 3B in Chapter 7).

(9) A study of the distribution of material expenditure among the Faculties reflects the priority attached to each Faculty by the sample libraries. AUL has allotted 75 percent of its material expenditure on Science and Technology, 19.5 percent on Arts, 4 percent on Oriental Languages and Linguistics and 1.5 percent on Education, while MKUL has devoted 50 percent for Arts, 44 percent for Science and Technology, 5 percent for OL & Linguistics and 1 percent for Education.* The priority given to the Faculties of S & T, followed by Arts in both the libraries may be explained by the need to cope with the introduction of increasing number of job-oriented courses in the Faculties of S & T, besides the socially relevant courses in the Faculty of Arts in recent years, consequent on the changes in the National Educational Policy (vide Table 4B in Chapter 7).

(10) When comparing the growth rate of material expenditure of the sample libraries with that of the standards suggested by EhikhamenoF, it is found that both AUL and MKUL have not satisfied these norms. In order to cope with the rapidly growing volumes and cost of publications, it is desirable that these libraries should maintain an annual growth rate of 10 to 15 percent at least for their book-budget allocation (vide Table 4C in Chapter 7).

(11) A comparative analysis of the material expenditure on each Faculty by the sample libraries indicates that MKUL

* The greater allotment on S & T in AUL is accounted for by the existence of a large number of courses in the Faculty of S & T, whereas in MKUL, the allotment of 50 percent to the Faculty of Arts may be explained by the availability of majority of courses in the Faculty of Arts.

has spent a larger amount of funds on Arts (Rs. 94.53 lakhs) than AUL (Rs. 25.61 lakhs) over the plan periods. Contrary to this, AUL has reserved relatively a larger share to S &T (Rs. 1 crore) than that of MKUL (Rs. 82.84 lakhs) in order to meet the demands of the students of the newly introduced courses in Agriculture, Engineering and Medical Sciences. In the case of OL & Linguistics, the amount spent by MKUL is higher in all the plan periods except the 5 plan. Only during this period, AUL has received special grants, due tothe upgradation of the Department of Linguistics as a Centre of Advanced Study. There is no marked difference in the material expenditure of both the libraries on Education (vide Table 4D in Chapter 7).

(12) A further analysis of the book expenditure among the Faculties given in Table 5A reveals that AUL has committed 70.9 percent for S & T, 22.4 percent for Arts, 4.8. percent for OL& Linguistics, and 1.9 percent for Education. Similarly, MKUL has allocated its book expenditure in the order of 50.7 percent for Arts, 43 percent for S & T, 5 percent for OL & Linguistics and 1.3 percent for Education during the plan periods.

(13) In the case of periodical expenditure (vide Table 6 in Chapter 7) AUL has distributed a larger proportion on S & T (82.5%) followed by Arts (12.7%), OL & Linguistics (3.1%) and Education (1.7%); whereas MKUL has contributed almost equal proportion on Arts (49.2%) and S& T (45.5%) followed by OL & Linguistics (4.5%) and Education (2.8%).

(14) The ratio of books and periodical expenditure has shown a decreasing trend in both the Libraries, as a result of larger contribution to the subscription of periodicals from the V plan onwards. In AUL, the ratio has declined from

4:1 to 3:1 in the Faculty of Arts, from 2:1 to 1:1 in the Faculty of S & T, from 7:1 to 3:1 in the Faculty of OL & Linguistics and from 6:1 to 3:1 in Education. In MKUL, the ratio has narrowed down from 3:1 to 1:1 in the Faculty of Arts, from 4:1 to 1:1 in S & T, from 3:1 to 2:1 in OL & Linguistics and from 4:1 to 2:1 in Education.

(15) Comparatively, MKUL has spent more on periodicals than AUL. But both the libraries have spent larger amount on S & T, responding to the focus given by the National Educational policy and the escalation of periodical costs in recent times. However, when comparing the book and periodical expenditure with the standards of Koch and Randall, both the libraries have not satisfied the prescribed standards. Therefore, it is desirable that the proportion of amount allotted for the subscription of periodicals has to be increased to the level suggested in order to meet the growing demands.

(16) An analysis of the size of the library collection in the sample libraries indicates that AUL has got larger collections of 3.11 lakhs volumes than that of MKUL with 2.16 lakhs volumes. But the rate of additions in the MKUL has shown a significant increase (7.2 fold) than that of (2 fold increase) % AUL. The growth rate of additions in both the libraries is higher in the VI plan, than the previous plan periods. This may be due to the stress on education and human resource development initiated by the Government during the VI plan (Table 10). But when compared with the standards suggested by Randall, only MKUL has fulfilled the criteria of 6-10 percent annual additions to the total stock during the last two plan periods.

(17) A study of the composition of the Library collections indicates that books constitute 90 percent and periodicals 10 percent in both the libraries. But, the rate of additions

of books in the MKUL is greater (8 fold) than that of AUL (3 fold) (Table 11). This may be attributed to the fact that MKUL, functioning since

(18) The late sixtees has concentrated more on strengthening its book collection to suit the multifarious instructional programmes of the University. In the case of periodical % collection also, the annual average additions of MKUL is higher (4 fold) than AUL (1.3 fold) which may be due to the larger allotment of funds received by MKUL for the subscription of periodicals. The growth rate of periodicals in both the libraries has shown a significant increase only from the V plan onwards. This is meant to meet the demands, consequent on the introduction of M.Phil, programmes, increase in the enrollment of scholars and the insistence of the research degree for the staff members in both the Universities.

(19) The ratio of books and periodicals indicates that AUL has maintained a constant ratio of 7:1 while MKUL has registered a steep increase from 11:1 to 19:1 over the years, indicating probably the expansion of courses in the Faculty of Arts, which require more of books than of periodicals.

(20) The composition of library collections in the sample libraries reveals that among the collections of AUL 52 percent belongs to S & T, 33 percent Arts, 12 percent OL and Linguistics and 3 percent Education. In MKUL, 47 percent of the collections belong to Arts, 44 percent to S and T, 7 percent to OL and Linguistics and 2 percent to Education. The predominance of the library collection inthe Faculties of Arts, Science and Technology in both the libraries may be attributed to the growing number of Departments and students' population in these faculties (vide Table 12).

(21) An evaluation of the adequacy of the Book-budgets alloted to the sample libraries based on user population (cost per user) indicates that MKUL has been financed adequately to cope with the growing user population. While comparing the funds allotted with that of the relevant norms, it is evident that the book-budget of MKUL has far exceeded the norm throughout the plan periods. It is suggested that AUL may endeavour to obtain like enhanced grant so as to meet the needs of the continuously increasing user population (Table 13).

(22) An examination of the adequacy of the library collection based on the number of user strength (volume per user) indicates that in both the libraries, the volume per user has been increasing considerably during the study period.*

(23) Similarly, the attempt to assess the optimum size of the collections in the sample libraries based on possessing relevant/ useable collections, bring to light the fact that MKUL satisfies the absolute minimum 'use per volume' of one loan a year in all the plan periods, while AUL has come close to this fixed norm (vide Table 15).

(24) The above analysis shows that AUL is yet to attain the standards of collection in terms of adequacy and effectiveness. Being a unitary residential university offering a wide variety of instructional and research programmes,** AUL needs much more funds sufficient

---

* In AUL, the volume per user has increased from 29 to 34, while in MKUL from 137 to 178. The disparity in the volume per user achievement between the AUL and MKUL may be accounted for by the fact that the student's enrollment in the courses conducted by the Departments of study of MKU is very much smaller than such enrollment in AU, as the latter is a residential teaching and research institution.

** There are about 44 departments in Annamalai University and there is an enrollment of 2500 Graduates, 1500 Post-graduates and 500 Researchers besides a staff strength of 950.

to meet all its curricular requirements. Presently AUL is getting only three percent allotment out of the University fund. In view of the rapidly growing student population, the commencement of professional courses and the rising cost of publications a provision of 20 percent* for the libraries from the University Budgets.

Processing Unit

(25) An analysis of the amount spent on the various input items of the processing units indicates that three-fourths of the total have been spent on the personnel and the residual on the other items. Totally during the study period AUL has invested Rs. 43 lakhs on the Processing Unit, out of which 75.5 percent has been spent on personnel; 9.3 percent on binding; 7.3 percent on raw materials; 3.4 percent on building; 3.1 percent on miscellaneous and 1.4 percent on furniture. As against this, out of the total of Rs. 6.26 lakhs,* MKUL has spent 76 percent for personnel; 13.2 percent for binding; 4.6 percent for raw materials; 3 percent for building; 2.5 percent for miscellaneous and 0.7 percent for furniture. Comparatively, the investment of MKUL on the processing unit is larger (Rs. 6.261 lakhs)* than that of AUL (Rs. 4.3 lakhs)* and the proportion of variation ranges from 15 percent to 59 percent.

(26) An examination of the output of the sample libraries sheds light on the fact that AUL has processed 69700* volumes and prepared 3.49* lakhs of catalogue cards as against MKUL which has processed 56700 volumes and prepared 2.02 lakhs of cards during the study period. In monetary terms also the output of AUL is higher (Rs. 55047) than

---

* The time has now come to reconsider the recommendation of the Kothari Commission of 10 percent, and to improve this percentage of expenditure on libraries. Prof. K.N. Raj Committee has also recommended 20 percent of University Budget to be allotted in the case of the Karnataka University Libraries.

that of MKUL (Rs. 45367).The productivity of the respective Technical Units also confirms the above result, which implies the better productivity of the Technical Unit of AUL when compared with the Technical Unit of MKUL.

(27) An analysis of the Unit cost of the technical services indicates that both the libraries have achieved. unit cost by processing maximum number of volumes. AUL has processed a volume at the cost of Rs. 5.68, while MKUL at Rs.10.3 over the plan periods. Therefore, the economy of processing in AUL is greater than that of MKUL. This may be attributed to the greater turnover in the processing unit of AUL. In order to minimise the unit cost of processing, MKUL has to increase the number of volumes processed per plan period.

(28) A study of the impact of technical services on circulation reveals that there is a positive correlation between the number of volumes processed (X) and the number of volumes circulated (Y). From the 'R' value it is identified that the number of volumes processed has influenced circulation by 57 percent in AUL and 99 percent in MKUL. Hence it is understood that MKUL is able to expedite the circulation service more than AUL, which again is due to the practice of 'Open-Access' system and the availability of efficient collection Service Unit.

(29) An analysis of the amount allotted to the Service Unit indicates that labour has consumed a major share and the rest has been allotted among the other items. From the total allotment of Rs. 2.6 lakhs* to the Service Unit of AUL, 71.1 percent has been spent on the personnel, 16.7 percent on space, 7 percent on furniture and 5.2 percent on the miscellaneous items. In the same way, from the total of Rs. 4.3 lakhs allotted for the Service Unit of MKUL, 79.8 percent has been spent for personnel, 13.5

* Geometric mean

percent for space, 3.6 percent for miscellaneous items and 3.1 percent for furniture. The total allotment in the MKUL is higher than that of AUL and the amount of variation is Rs. 1.7 lakhs.*

(30) The personnel cost of the sample libraries has shown a rising trend during the period under review. It has increased from 40 percent to 89.8 percent in AUL and from 54.8 percent to 89.8 percent in MKUL. This again is attributed to the growing demand for sufficient work force in the service unit to render the expected level of service. The proportion of amount allotted to the non-recurring items such as space and furniture has declined.** However the amount spent by MKUL on personnel, space, furniture and miscellaneous items has been higher than that of AUL, which may be explained by the receipt of larger funds (by way of grants).

(31) A study of the outputs of the two libraries indicates that AUL has recorded a total circulation of 6.96 lakhs volumes over the plan periods, as against MKUL which has circulated 6.34 lakhs volumes. Similarly, the total number of reference queries answered in AUL has been greater (8.4 lakhs) than that of MKUL (6.02 lakhs).

(32) Consequently, AUL has been able to provide maximum service with least cost. The cost per circulation of AUL is Rs. 0.37 as against Rs. 0.6 in MKUL. In the case of reference service also, the cost per unit is Rs. 0.31 in AUL and Rs. 0.77 in MKUL. The minimum unit cost achieved by A UL is attributed to the efficient and co-ordinated functioning of the service unit.

---

* Geometric mean

** In the case of non-recurring items only the depreciation value has been taken into consideration.

(33) The application of the Benefit-cost-ratio of the services in the sample libraries reveals that the marginal output obtained is more than the marginal cost incurred in both the libraries throughout the plan periods.

(34) The MC of AUL is Rs. 84,000 while that of MB from circulation is 2.25 lakhs and reference queries answered is 2.4 lakhs.

The BCR, therefore, works out to 2.7 and 3.7 respectively for the circulation and reference services over the plan periods in AUL.

As against this, in MKUL, the MC is Rs.1.3 lakhs and the MB from the circulation is 2.7 lakhs and from the reference service is 3.5 lakhs. Hence, the BCR in MKUL works out to 1.8 for both the services. Comparatively, the BCR for the AUL is higher than that of MKUL. This is attributed to the better organised functioning of the service unit and the larger number of user population in AUL.

(35) An analysis of the performance efficiency of the service units in both the libraries has shown that AUL has invested a sum of Rs. 2.59 lakhs over the service unit and the number of volumes utilised amounted to 15.3 lakhs. Its efficiency ratio when computed is 5.9. As against this, MKUL has invested a sum of Rs. 4.3 lakhs and the return from the service unit amounts to 12.36 lakhs of volumes and therefore it has attained an efficiency ratio of 2.9 only. Comparatively, the efficiency of the Service Unit of AUL seems to be higher than that of the MKUL. This points to the need for well organised service to the users to be attempted by the Service Unit of the MKUL which may contribute to improve the efficiency ratio.

(36) The performance measure of the total library activities is calculated by dividing the total document exposure hours

by the total user population. It is found out that the total document exposure hours of AUL is higher than that of MKUL and the proportion of variation ranges from 82 percent to 93 percent. This is explained by the fact that the utility of AUL is tremendously larger than MKUL* (99%). As Annamalai University is a residential institution, the students enjoy easy access to the library and this would have improved the utilisation of library to a greater extent than the MKUL.

MKUL is situated 80 KM away from the heart of the city and the distance factor deters (most of the time) the readers who reside in the city from using it more frequently. Hence, the document exposure is found to be less in MKUL.

(37) When analysing the factors contributing to the total output (circulation) of the library services, it is found that in both the libraries the influences of the fund allocation, the material collection and the user population are marked (97% in AUL and 99% in MKUL) on the outputs. Among these three variables, the influence of the user population is found to be greater followed by the collection size and the total investment in the case of both the libraries.

Therefore, it may be concluded on the basis of the above findings that the performance of the acquisition unit of the MKUL is noteworthy and effective. It may be due to the steady flow of adequate funds and the careful selection of the material input based on the user needs. The inadequate allotment of finance, the constant increase in the user population and the introduction of new courses in AUL seem to have affected adversely the performance of this unit. This situation can be easily rectified by adopting the technique of perspective planning. For the acquisition unit, taking into account the programmes of the institution, user-population and the quantum of research activities.

A long term planning in all respects staff, books and periodicals library services, building and other items can be prepared well in advance and can be linked with the price index numbers of the country for annual adjustments.

On the other hand, the performance of the processing unit of AUL has not only been efficient but also effective which indicates maximum output as well as the minimum cost-input for the performance. This may be attributed to the efficient functioning of the technical unit in AUL. In order to improve the output of the technical unit of the MKUL, it has to develop further its manpower input. In the same way, the Benefit-cost ratio of the service unit of the AUL is found to be higher than that of the Service unit of MKUL, which indicates the prompt and efficient service of the Service unit of AUL.

Appendix

An user's survey of the scholars of the Annamalai University undertaken by the researcher for her M. Phil study during 1984-85 has been based on collecting the primary data from the Library users of the various faculties. One of the major objectives of this study is to identify the users assessment of the existing library collection and services of the AUL. The research scholars opinion regarding the library collection is tabulated below:

Table1
Opinion of the Researchers about the Library Collection in AUL

Research Scholars	*Satisfied*		*. Moderately Satisfied*		*Not at all Satisfied*	
Science	5	(8%)	2	(3%)	19	(30%)
Arts	5	(8%)	2	(3%)	19	(30%)
Education	1	(2 %)	2	(3%)	5	(8%)
Languages	1	(2%)	1	(2%)	1	(2%)
Total	12	(20%)	7	(10%)	4.5	70%

The above table shows that there searchers seem to desire (i) a separate research collection, (ii) adequate, journals in their subjects, (iii) adequate text and reference books and (iv) promptness in the procurement of documents. The factors which deterred the development of a comprehensive and adequate collections have been identified as (i) escalation of costs of books and periodicals (ii) inadequate financial provision etc.

With the view to improve the technical services, the scholars' opinion about the classification and cataloguing systems followed in AUL have been collected and presented below:

Table 2
Research Scholars' Opinion of the Classification System in AUL

Research scholars	*Satisfied*	*Moderately satisfied*	*Not at all satisfied*
Science	19 (30%)	5 (8%)	3 (5%)
Arts	8 (12%)	8 (12%)	5 (7%)
Education	7 (11%)	2 (3%)	-
Languages	5 (8%)	1 (2%)	1 (2%)
Total	39 (61%)	16 (25%)	

From the above table it is discernible that only 14 percent of the scholars have been found to be dissatisfied with the present classification system. Others have expressed their satisfaction regarding the helpfulness of the system. Similarly, the cataloguing system followed in AUL has been collected and presented in the following table.

From the table it is identified that more than 70 percent of the scholars are found to be satisfied with the cataloguing practices in AUL.

The scholars were asked to comment on the services rendered by the staff members of the reference section in the AUL. Their responses have been tabulated below:

It is evident from the following table that nearly 60 percent of the scholars have been satisfied with the services rendered

Table 3
Research Scholars' Opinion of the Cataloguing System in AUL

Researchers	*Helpful*	*Moderately Helpful*	*Not at all helpful*
Science	19 (29%)	2 (3%)	6 (0%)
Arts	12 (19%)	1 (2%)	8 (12%)
Education	7 (11%)	1 (2%)	1 (2%)
Languages	4 (6%)	(7%)	3 (5%)
Total	(65%)	(7%)	15 (28%)

Table 4
Research Scholars' Opinion about the Services Rendered by the Staff in the Reference Department

Researchers	*Satisfied*	*Moderately Satisfied*	*Not at all satisfied*
Science	17 (26%)	2 (3%)	8 (12%)
Arts	6 (9%)	1 (2 %)	14 (22%)
Education	7 (11%)	1 (2%)	1 (2%)
Languages	4 (6%)	-	3 (5%)
Total	34 (53%)	4 (7%)	26 (41%)

by the staff members in the reference section. Others have expressed the need for additional staff members, well trained in information handling and organising intensified information services.

An attempt has also been made to find out (i) the adequacy of the (material) resources, (ii) the helpfulness of the technical services of the Madurai Kamaraj University Library by collecting information from thirty research scholars belonging to various faculties. The respondents were asked to give their remarks about the collection of MKUL. Their responses have been collected and tabulated below:

Table 5

Opinion of the Research Scholars about the Library Collection in MKUL

Research scholars	*Satisfied*	*Moderately satisfied*	*Not at all satisfied*
Science	9 (30%)		1 (3.5%)
Arts	9 30%)	-	1 (3.5%)
Education	3 (10%)	1 (3%)	1 (3.5%)
Languages	3 (10%)	1 (3%)	1 (3.5%)
Total	25 (80%)	2 (6%)	

It is noticed from the above table that most of the respondents (80%) are of the opinion that the collection of MKUL is satisfactory. Some of them expressed that reference collection is not up-to-date and a few pointed out the inadequacy in the collection of back volumes of periodicals. In general, the information sources available in the MKUL are found to be fairly adequate and satisfactory in meeting the specific and general information needs of the students, researchers and staff members of the University.

In order to assess the usefulness of the Technical Services in MKUL, users' opinion have been gathered. The following table illustrates the users' view regarding the classification system followed in MKUL.

Table 6
Research Scholars Opinion of the Classification System in MKUL

Research scholars	*Satisfied*	*Moderately satisfied*	*Not at all satisfied*
Science	8 (26.5 %)	-	2 (7%)
Arts	8 (26.5%)	-	2 (7%)
Education	3 (10%)	1 (3%)	1 (3%)
Languages	2 (7%)	2 (7%)	1 (3%)
Total	21 (70%)	3 (10 %)	6 (20%)

It is observed from the above table that nearly 70 percent of the users are satisfied with the clasasification system followed in MKUL. Others have experienced difficulty in following the system due to the intricacy of the notation. In general, majority of the users are satisfied with the classification practices in MKUL.

Similarly, the helpfulness of the cataloguing system in MKUL has been assessed by collecting the opinion of the research scholars. Their responses have been tabulated below:

It is clear from the above table that nearly 60 percent of the researchers have been satisfied with the cataloguing practices followed in MKUL. Others have felt that the information contained in the entries are not adequate. In other words, they are not very much helpful to get a complete picture of the documents.

The respondents were asked to give their opinions regarding the services of the reference section. Their responses are tabulated below:

Table 7
Research Scholars Opinion about the Cataloguing System in MKUL

Research Scholars	*Helpful*	*Moderately Helpful*	*Not at all Helpful*
Science	6 (21%)	3 (10)	1 (3.3 %)
Arts	7 (25%)	1 (3.3)	2 (7%)
Education	2 (7 %0	1 (3.3)	1 (3.3%)
Languages	2 (7%)	1 (3.3)	2 (7 %)
Total	17 (60%)	6 (20%)	6 (20%)

It is observed from the above table that nearly 60 percent of the users have been satisfied with the services of the reference department of MKUL. Others have commented that the number of staff members are not only limited but also not properly trained to offer specialised information services.

Research Scholars	*Satisfied*	*Moderately Satisfied*	*Not at all Satisfied*
Science	7 (23%)	-	3 (10%)
Arts	5 (16%)	2 (7%)	3 (10%)
Education	3 (10%)	-	2 (7%)

Bibliography

Books

1. Ahmad, Nazir. *University Library Practices in Developing Countries*. London: KPI, 1984.

2. Association of Indian Universities. *National Policy on University Libraries: Report,* New Delhi; AIU, 1985.

3. Association of Indian Universities. *Universities Handbook (1985-86): Diamond Jubilee Edition.* New Delhi: AIU, 1985.

4. Blagden, John Frederick. *Do We Really need Libraries.* London: Clive Bingley, 1980.

5. Buckland, Michael Keeble, *Book Availability and the Library User.* New York: Pergamon Press, 1975.

6. Childers, Thomas."Statistics that describe libraries and library Service". *Advances in Librarianship,* Vol. 5. New York: Academic Press, 1976.

7. Chou,Ya-Jun. *Statistical Analysis.* New York: Holt, Rinehart and Winston, 1969.

8. Cline, Hugh F. *Building Library Collections.* Toronto: D.C. Heath and Company, 1981.

9. Cowley, John. *The Management of Polytechnic Libraries.* London: Gower Publishing Company, 1985.

10. De Prospo, Ernest R. et al. *Performance Measures for Public Libraries.* Chicago: ALA Public Library Association, 1973.

11. Dongerkey, SR."Libraries in University Education".In: N.N. Gidwani (Ed.) *Comparative Librarianship.* Delhi: Vikas, 1973.

12. Evan, E. et al. "Review of criteria used to measure Library effectiveness". In: Rcss Shimmon (Ed.) *A Reader in Library Management,* London: Clive Bingley, 1976.

13. Fabricant, S. *A Primer on Productivity.* New York: Random House, 1968.

14. Grieder, Theodore. *Acquisitions: Where, What and How.* Westport: Greenwood Press, 1978.

15. Gelfand, MA. *University Libraries for Developing Countries.* New Delhi: Universal Book Co., 1974.

16. Guha, AK and Jayaswal, PL."Budget Management in libraries for higher education in Delhi: A comparative study". In: S.K. Kapoor et al (Eds.) *Application of Management Techniques to Library and Information Systems.* Calcutta: IASLIC, 1979.

17. Helal, Ahmed H. "Approaches to the evaluation of Technical Services in Libraries". In: Lancaster, F W and Cleverdon, CW (Eds.) *Evaluation and Scientific Management of Libraries and Information Centres,* Noordhoff-Leydon, 1977.

18. Hamburg, M. et al. *Library Planning and Decision Making Systems.* Cambridge, MA: M.I.T. Press, 1974.

19. Hayes, RM and Becker, J. "Cost accounting in Libraries". In: Handbook of data processing for libraries. New York: Wiley/Becker - Hayes, 1970.

20. Lancaster, FW. Information Retrieval systems: Characteristics, Testing and Evaluation. New York: John Wiley and Sons, 1979.

21. Lynden, Frederick C."Library Materials Budgeting in the private University Library: Austerity and Action". *Advances in Librarianship,* Vol. 10, New York: Academic Press, 1980.

22. Marchant, Maurice P. *Participative Management in Academic Libraries.* Westport: Greenwood Press, 1976.

23. Martyn, 3. and Lancaster, FW. *Investigative Methods in Library and Information Secience: an Introduction* Virginia: Information Resources Press, 1981.

24. Ministry of Education, India. *Challenge of Education: a Policy Perspective.* New Delhi:Ministry of Education, 1985.

25. Oldman, Christine."Demonstrating library value: a report of a research investigation". In: Vaughan, Anthony (Ed.). *Studies in library Management.* Vol.7, London: Ciive Bingley, 1982.

26. Osborn, Charles B. *Academic Research and Library Resources.* London: Greenwood Press,1976.

Raffel, JA and Shishko, R. *Systematic Analysis of University Libraries: An Application of Cost-Benefit Analysis tc the M.I.T. Libraries.* Cambridge: The M.I.T. Press, 1969.

28. Roberts, Stephen A. *Cost Management for Library and Information Services.*London: Butterworths, 1955.

29. Rowe, D. "Application of the Theory of the Firm to Library costing". In:Roberts, Stephen A.(Ed.) *Costing and the Economics of Library and Information Services,* Aslib Reader Series, Vol. 5, London: Aslib, 1984.

30. Srivastava, S Wand Verma SK. *University Libraries in India.* New Delhi: Sterling Publishers, 1980.

31. Shimon, Ross. *A Reader in Library Management,* London: Clive Bingley, 1976.

32. Tejomurty, A. *Studies in Academic Librarianship,* Jaipur: Printwell, 1987.

33. Trumpeter, Margo C. *Basic Budgeting Practices for Librarians.* Chicago: American Library Association, 1985.

34. Turtle, Helen Welch. "Standards for Technical Service Cost Studies". *Advances in Librarianship,* Vol. 1, New York: Academic Press, 1970.

35. University Education Commission (1948-49). *Report.* New Delhi Manager of Publications, GOI, 1949.

36. University Education Commission (1964-66). *Educational Planning and the National Policy.* New Delhi: NCERT, 1971.

37. University Grants Committee (India). *University and College Libraries.* New Delhi: UGC, 1965.

38. University Grants Committee (UK). *Capital Provision for University Libraries: Report of a Working Party.* London: HMSO, 1976.

39. Waldhart, TJ and Marcum, TP. "Productivity measurement in academic libraries". *Advances in Librarianship,* Vol. 6. New York: Academic Press, 1976.

40. Wilson, TD. "The Evaluation of Bibliographical Resources". In: Lancaster, FW and Cleverdon, CW (Eds.) *Evaluation and Scientific Management of Libraries and Information Centres.* Noordhoff Leydon, 1977.

41. Wilson, LR and Tauber, MF. *The University Library.* New York: Columbia Press, 1956.

Journals

1. American Library Association. Association of College and Research Libraries. Draft: Standards for College libraries, 1975 Revision. *College and Research Libraries News 11,* Nov. 1974, pp. 284-305.

2. Arora, Sant R. and Paul, Rameshwar, N."Acquisition of Library materials: Aquantitative approach". In: *American Society for Information Science,* Proceedings, San Francisco, Westport, Conn., and London: Greenwood, 1969, pp. 495-499.

3. Bonn, George. "Evaluation of the Collection". *Library Trends,* Jan. 1974, pp. 265-303.

4. Brutcher, Constance."Cost-accounting for Library". *LRTS,* Vol. 8, No. 4, Fall 1964, pp. 413-417.

5. Burton, Robert E. "Formula Budgeting; An Example". *Special Libraries,* Feb. 1975, pp. 61-67.

6. Clapp, VW and Jordan, RT. "Quantitative criteria for Adequacy of Academic Library Collections". *College and Research Libraries,* Vol. 26, No. 5, Sep. 1965, pp. 371-380.

7. De Gennaro, R. "Austerity, technology and resource sharing: research libraries face the future". *Library Journal,* 100, 1975, pp. 917-923.

8. De Vleeschauwer, HJ. University Library: Its Nature and Functions" *Mousion,* Vol. 59, 1963, pp. 35-67.

9. Downs, PR and Heusman, JW. "Standards for University Libraries". *College and Research Libraries.* Vol. 31, No. l, Jan.1970, pp. 28-35.

10. Drake, Miriam A."Attribution of Library Costs". *College and Research Libraries,* Nov. 1977, pp. 514-519.

11. Duchesne, Roderick M. "Analysis of Costs and Performance". *Library Trends,* April, 1973, pp. 587-603.

12. Dumont, RR and Dumont PF. "Measuring library effectiveness". *Advances in Librarianship,* Vol. 9, 1979, pp. 104-141.

13. Ehikhamenor, Fabian A. "A Formula for allocating book funds : The search for simplicity and flexibility". *Libri,* Vol. 33, No. 2, 1983, pp. 148-161.

14. Fasana, PJ and Fall, JE. "Processing Costs for Science Monographs in the Columbia University Libraries". *LRTS,* Vol. 11, No. l, Winter 1967, pp. 97-114.

15. Gold, Steven D. "Allocating the book budget : An economic model". *College and Research Libraries,* Sept. 1975, pp. 397-402.

16. Goyal, SK. "Allocation of library funds to different departments of a University : an operational research approach". *College and Research Libraries,* May 1973, pp. 219-222.

17. Hamburg, M et al. "Library objectives and performance measures and their use in decision-making". *Library Quarterly,* Vol. 42, 1972, pp. 107-123.

18. Hannabuss, Stuart. "The concept of performance: a semantic review". *Aslib Proceedings,* Vol. 39, No. 5, 1987, pp. 149-158.

19. Hayes, RM and Borko, BH."Mathematical models of Information system use". *Information Processing and Management.* Vol. 19, No. 3, 1983, pp. 187-190.

20. Hindustan Times, 17.7.72.

21. Humphreys, KN. "Standards inUniversity Libraries". *Libri,* Vol. 20, No. 1-2,1970, pp.144-155.

22. Ifidon, Sam E. "Establishment of standards forbookstock in West African University Libraries". *Libri,* Vol. 33, No. 2, 1983, pp. 92-106.

23. Kantor, Paul B. "Evaluation and Feedback". *Annual Review of Library and Information Science.* Vol. 4, 1981, pp. 100-120.

24. Klintoe, K. "Cost analysis of technical information Unit". *Aslib Proceedings.* Vol. 27, No. 7, July 1971, pp. 362-371.

25. Knightly, John J, "Overcoming the criterion problem in the evaluation of library performance". *Special Libraries,* Vol. 70, No. 4, April 1979, pp. 173-178.

26. Koch, Hans-Albrecht. "Research on budgeting and standard for academic libraries in the Federal Republic of Germany. *Journal of Librarianship,* Vol. 17, No. 4, Oct. 1985, pp. 268-291.

27. Kohut, Joseph J. "Allocating the Book-Budget: A model". *College and Research Libraries.* May 1974, pp. 192-218.

28. Ladendorf, Janice, "Information Service evaluation: The gap between the ideal and the possible". *Special Libraries,* Vol. 64, No. 7, July 1973, pp. 273-279.

29. Lancaster, FW and Climenson, WD. "Evaluating the economic efficiency of a document retrieval system". *Journal of Documentation,* Vol. 24, No. 1, March 1968, pp. 16-25.

30. Leimkuhler, F and Cooper, Michael D."Cost Accounting and Analysis for University Libraries". *College and Research Libraries,* Vol. 36, No. 6, Nov. 1978.

31. Levine, MM. "The Circulation/Acquisition Ratio: An Input-Output Measure for Libraries". *Information Processing and Management.* Vol. 16, 1980, pp. 313-318.

32. Lewis, "Bibliographic Materials Fund Allocation". *Collection Development.* Vol. 6, No. 3/4, Fall/Winter, 1984, pp. 37-47.

33. Lipetz, Ben-Ami. "The evaluation of communication systems: some thoughts on effectiveness". *Science and Technology News,* Winter 1966, pp. 110-113.

34. Lynch, Beverly P. "University Library Standards". *Library Trends,* Summer 1982, pp. 33-47.

35. Maier, Joan M. "Analyzing Acquisitions and Cataloguing Costs". *LRTS,* Vol. 13, No. 1, Winter 1969, pp. 127-135.

36. MeGrath,William E. "A Pragmatic Book Allocation Formula for Academic and Public Libraries: With a test for its effectiveness. *LRTS,* Vol. 11, No. 4, Fall 1975, pp. 357-369.

37. Misra, VN and Phadke, DN. "Study on unit costing of Technical Processing in an academic library". Papers presented at the *XII IASLIC National Seminar,* Varanasi, December 28-31, 1986, pp. 55-67.

38. Morse, PM. "Measures of library effectiveness". *Library Quarterly,* Vol. 42, 1972, pp. 15-30.

39. Peep L and Sinkevicins K. "Financing system of USSR University Libraries". *College and Research Libraries,* May 1974, pp. 178-183.

40. Pings, Vern M. "Development of Quantitative Assessment of Medical Libraries". *College and Research Libraries,* Sep. 1968, pp. 373-381.

41. Randall, Gorden E. "Budgeting for Libraries". *Special Libraries,* Vol. 67, Jan. 1976, pp. 8-12.

42. Ranganathan, SR. "University Libraries Then and Now". *Library Herald,* Vol. 6, 1963, pp. 63-70.

43. Ranganathan, SR. "Academic Library System: Fourth Plan Period". *Library Science with a Slant to Documentation,* Vol. 2, No. 4, Dec. 1965, pp. 227-235.

44. Revill,D."Availability as a Performance Measure for Academic Libraries". *Journal of Librarianship,* Vol. 19, No. l, Jan. 1987, pp. 14-29.

45. Rouse, William B. "Optimal Resource Allocation in Library Systems". *Journal of the American Society for Information Science,* May-June 1975, pp. 157-165.

46. Rzasa,Philip V and Baker, Norman R. "Measures of effectiveness for a University Library". *Journal of the American Society for Information Science,* July-August 1972, pp. 248-253.

47. Sewell, PH. "The evaluation of library services in depth". *Unesco Bulletin for Libraries,* Vol. 22, Nov.-Dec. 1968, pp. 274-280.

48. Standera, Old rich R. "Cost and Effectiveness in the evaluation of an Information System: A case study. *Journal of the American Society for information Science,* Vol. 25, No. 3, May-June 1974, pp. 203-207.

49. Stoljarov̌, JN. "Optimum Size of Public Library Stocks". *UNESCO Bulletin for Libraries,* Vol. 7, Jan.-Feb. 1973, pp. 22-28.

50. Stubbs, Kendon. "University Libraries: Standards and Statistics", *College and Research Libraries,* Nov. 1981, pp. 527-538.

51. Suriya, M and Malathi, N. "Cost effectiveness of Library and Information Services: A Case study of Marine Biological Centre of Annamalai University. *XXXII All-India Library Conference,* SK University, Anantapur (AP), January 3-6, 1987.

52. Suriya, M and Malathi, N."University Libraries as economic systems" *Annals of Library Science and Documentation,* March 1987.

53. Suriya, M and Malathi, N. "Cost-Accounting of University Library system with reference to Tamil University Library, Thanjavur". *IASLIC Bulletin,* Vol. 32, No. 2, 1987, pp. 51-60.

54. Suriya, M and Kalavathi, MS. "Productivity Measurement in Academic Libraries". *Journal of Library and Information Science,* Vol. 12, No. l, June 1987, pp. 53-65.

55. Suriya, M and Kalavathi, S. "Measuring Library effectiveness: an evaluation". *Annals of Library Science and Documentation,* March 1988.

56. Suriya, M. and Kalavathi, MS. "Evaluating the Effectiveness of Technical Services in an academic library: A case Study". *IASLIC Bulletin,* 1988.

57. Suriya, M. and Kalavathy, MS. "Study of efficiency of Technical section of the Annamalai University Library". *Journal of Annamalai University,* Vol. 33, 1987.

58. Suriya, M. and Kalavathi, MS."Availability as a measure for evaluating the performance efficiency of an academic

library". *XXXIV All India Library Conference,* Calcutta, December, 20-23, 1.

59. Suriya, M and Kalavathy, MS. "Evaluation of Collection effectiveness in University Library: A case study". *XXXIV All India Library Conference,* Calcutta, December 20-23, 1988.

60. Van House, Nancy A. "Public Library Effectiveness: Theory, Measures and Determinants". *LISR,* Vol. 8, 1986, pp. 261-283.

61. Watkins, David R. *"Standards for University Libraries", Library Trends,* Oct. 1972, pp. 190-203.

62. Welwood, RJ."Book-Budget Allocation: An objective formula for the small academic library", *Canadian Library Journal,* Vol. 34, No. 3, 1977, pp. 213-219.

63. Wessel, CJ. "Criteria for evaluating technical library effectiveness". *Aslib Proceedings,* Vol. 20, No. 1, Nov. 1968.

64. Zweizig, Douglas L. "Measuring Library use". *Drexel Library Quarterly,* Vol. 13, No. 3, July 1977, pp. 3-15.

Index